ONE IN 2000?

ONE
IN
2000?

Towards Catholic-Orthodox Unity

Agreed Statements and Parish Papers

Edited by
PAUL McPARTLAN

ST PAULS

St Pauls
Middlegreen, Slough SL3 6BT, United Kingdom
Moyglare Road, Maynooth, Co. Kildare, Ireland

© St Pauls 1993

ISBN 085439 439 7

Printed by The Guernsey Press Co. Ltd, Guernsey, C.I.

St Pauls is an activity of the priests and brothers of the Society of St Paul
who proclaim the Gospel through the media of social communication

Contents

Foreword   7

Preface   9

AGREED STATEMENTS

The Theological Dialogue between
the Catholic Church and the Orthodox Church
Monsignor Eleuterio Fortino   15

The Mystery of the Church and of the Eucharist
in the Light of the Mystery of the Holy Trinity
(Munich, 1982)   37

Faith, Sacraments and the Unity of the Church
(Bari, 1987)   53

The Sacrament of Order in the Sacramental
Structure of the Church
(Valamo, 1988)   71

PARISH PAPERS

The Prayer of the Heart: East and West
Sister Pamela Hayes, RSCJ   89

How Two Worlds Drifted Apart
Canon Hugh Wybrew   101

Regaining our Lost Unity
Father Paul McPartlan 117

Praying with Icons
Bishop Kallistos of Diokleia 141

Contributors 169

APPENDIX

Letter of His Holiness Pope John Paul II
to the Bishops of Europe on relations between
Catholics and Orthodox in the new situation of
Central and Eastern Europe
(31 May, 1991) 173

Foreword

The will of our Lord that his disciples throughout the centuries should be one, as he and his Father are one, has not always been fulfilled in the Church's long history. Divisions have often occurred among Christians, some of them temporary, some still lasting and, for that reason, more serious. Such is the great schism that took place in 1054 between the Churches of Rome and Constantinople.

This great schism has led the Churches of the West and of the East into a long and deep alienation from one another. The consequences have been tragic. The two sides have engaged in polemic with each other and, what is even worse, have lost the benefit of each other's spiritual and theological charisms which they shared in the first centuries.

It is in our own time that this course has been reversed thanks to the bold and historic steps taken by Pope Paul VI and the Ecumenical Patriarch of Constantinople, Athenagoras I, who decided to initiate a 'dialogue of love' between the two Churches, to be followed by an official 'dialogue of truth' between them. Following in their steps, their successors, Pope John Paul II and Ecumenical Patriarch Dimitrios I, gave their own blessing and an official theological dialogue began in 1980.

The present book, edited by a young Roman Catholic theologian who has a profound knowledge of both Roman Catholic and Orthodox theology, as well as a deep devotion to the cause of the Church's unity, constitutes a valuable contribution to the ongoing theological rapprochement between the Roman Catholic and the Orthodox Churches. In its first part, it makes available to the English speaking public the texts agreed upon up to now by the two sides in the theological dialogue, while in its second part it offers a selection of important papers by Roman Catholic and Orthodox authors, originally given in a course organised in the Roman Catholic parish of Our Lady of Victories on Kensington High Street in London. In both parts of the book, the reader will find very valuable material to be acquainted with, enabling an assessment of the present state of the theological rapprochement between Roman Catholicism and Orthodoxy. Reading this book, one cannot but be grateful to our Lord for the progress achieved so far and pray to him for a successful conclusion to this process.

It is only God, through his Holy Spirit, who can lead the two Churches to full communion. But it is our task to work with all our strength for the coming of that day. We cannot but rejoice at the positive signs contained in this book and thank the editor and the authors for offering this service to the Church of God.

+ John (Zizioulas)
Metropolitan of Pergamon

Preface

Gathered to celebrate the feast of the apostle Andrew, patron of the Ecumenical Patriarchate, at the Phanar in Istanbul on 30 November, 1979, Pope John Paul II and Patriarch Dimitrios I announced the establishment of a Joint Commission to begin theological dialogue between the Orthodox Church and the Roman Catholic Church. The Pope memorably set a target for the work of this commission.

> 'Is it not time to hasten towards perfectly brotherly reconciliation, so that the dawn of the third millennium may find us standing side by side, in full communion, to bear witness together to salvation before the world, the evangelisation of which is waiting for this sign of unity?'[1]

The countdown to the year 2000 has now begun in earnest. We have entered the final ten years, proclaimed as a Decade of Evangelisation. Such a venture should, in any case, prompt renewed ecumenical endeavour, given the fundamental link between Christian unity and the spread of the Good News: 'Father, may they all be one...so that the world may believe' (Jn 17:21). However, the fact that this particular ecumenical dialogue might not inconceivably be crowned with full communion by the year 2000, gives Catholics and Orthodox a unique incentive to pray, reflect and strive. The new political climate in Eastern Europe only further encourages dialogue between Catholics and Orthodox, all now enjoying the possibility of responding to the promptings of the Holy Spirit in freedom.

Lasting unity requires the interest and involvement not just of experts but of the general faithful in the dioceses and parishes of both Churches. It was with this in mind that an Autumn Course was held in the parish of Our Lady of Victories in Kensington, London, in 1990. The course bore the title: 'Towards the Year 2000: Catholic-Orthodox Unity?' and the four papers in the second part of this book were first delivered there to a parish audience of a hundred or so people.

This large response encouraged the thought that the papers might be of use to parish groups more widely, assisting discussion of the implications of unity and prompting a prayerful desire for it. The fact that the three agreed statements that the dialogue has produced have not all been available in a popular format has sadly restricted their impact upon the lives of communities in the two Churches. Publication of the course seemed an excellent opportunity to remove this obstacle by reproducing the statements, too, as the first part of this book, and allowing the parish papers to function, directly or indirectly, as commentaries upon them.

I am most grateful to Monsignor Eleuterio F. Fortino, Under-Secretary of the Pontifical Council for Promoting Christian Unity[2] and Co-Secretary of the Joint International Commission for Theological Dialogue between the Roman Catholic Church and the Orthodox Church, for contributing a particularly valuable article to introduce the agreed statements, and to Monsignor Kevin McDonald, of the same Pontifical Council, for translating it. Since Mgr Fortino ends his account with a quotation from the letter written by Pope John Paul II on 31 May, 1991, to the bishops of Europe on Catholic-Orthodox relations, it seemed opportune to include this letter as an Appendix to the present volume. There is, inevitably, a certain amount of overlap between Mgr Fortino's paper and my paper from the original parish course, which dealt with the same topic. However, since the two papers, in fact, largely complement one another, I have left my paper unchanged, apart from a few additional sentences to outline the most recent developments.

The text of the agreed statements exists originally in French[3] and Greek. For their publication here, I have used, with some revisions, the translations into English which first appeared in the *Information Service*[4] of the Pontifical Council for Promoting Christian Unity. Throughout, I have rendered 'church' with a small 'c' whenever the reference is clearly to a local church, i.e. a diocese, and with a capital 'C' in all other instances.

Many thanks are also due, of course, to my fellow authors of the individual papers, not least for the skill and enthusiasm with which they delivered the original parish talks.

Finally, I wish to thank the distinguished Orthodox theologian and founding member of the international Catholic-Orthodox dialogue, Metropolitan John of Pergamon, for kindly contributing a Foreword to this book, and also the Society of St John Chrysostom, whose generous financial support enabled its publication. The Society exists to make known to western Christians the history, worship and spirituality of eastern Christendom and to work and pray for the unity of all, especially East and West, in the one Church of Christ. Further details may be obtained from the Membership Secretary, Society of St John Chrysostom, Marian House, Holden Avenue, London N12 8HY.

I gratefully dedicate this volume to Canon Adrian Arrowsmith, Parish Priest of Our Lady of Victories, pastor and friend. May it be of service to many other parishes and groups, kindling an active desire for the blessed day when the Church will once again breathe with her two lungs,[5] the eastern and the western.

Paul McPartlan
6 August, 1992
Feast of the Transfiguration

NOTES

1. These words were recalled and reiterated by Cardinal Willebrands at the Phanar for the same feast in 1989; cf Pontifical Council for Promoting Christian Unity, *Information Service*, n.73, 1990 (II), p. 30.
2. The Secretariat for Promoting Christian Unity (hereafter, SPCU) became the Pontifical Council for Promoting Christian Unity (hereafter, PCPCU) in 1988.
3. 'Le Mystère de L'Eglise et de l'Eucharistie à la lumière du Mystère de la Sainte Trinité', original French text in *Irénikon* 55(1982), pp. 350-362; 'Foi, Sacrements et Unité de l'Eglise', *Irénikon* 60(1987), pp. 336-349; 'Le Sacrement de l'Ordre dans la Structure sacramentelle de l'Eglise en particulier l'importance de la succession apostolique pour la sanctification et l'unité du peuple de Dieu', *Irénikon* 61(1988), pp. 347-359.
4. 'The Mystery of the Church and of the Eucharist in the Light of the Mystery of the Holy Trinity', SPCU, *Information Service*, no. 49, 1982 (II/III), pp. 107-112; 'Faith, Sacraments and the Unity of the Church', SPCU, Information Service, n.64, 1987(II), pp. 82-87; 'The Sacrament of Order in the Sacramental Structure of the Church with particular reference to the importance of Apostolic Succession for the sanctification and unity of the People of God', SPCU, *Information Service*, no. 68, 1988(III-IV), pp. 173-178. The original texts of the second and third agreed statements contain the subtitles used in this volume. That of the first statement contains no subtitles; those used here are taken from the edition of the SPCU translation which appeared as a Catholic Truth Society pamphlet, number Do 553.
5. This image, coined by Yves Congar, has been used several times by Pope John Paul II; cf Y. Congar, *Diversity and Communion* (SCM, London, 1984), p. 89.

Agreed Statements

The Theological Dialogue between the Catholic Church and the Orthodox Church

Monsignor Eleuterio F. Fortino*

'The purpose of the dialogue between the Roman Catholic Church and the Orthodox Church is the reestablishment of full communion between these two Churches. This communion, based on unity of faith according to the common experience and tradition of the early Church, will find its expression in the common celebration of the Holy Eucharist.'

This explicit objective, stated in these terms in the preparatory document (see below), was established before the Catholic-Orthodox dialogue began. The clarity of the aim and the consequent methodology adopted already constitute an appreciable result of the fraternal relations that were progressively reestablished after the Second Vatican Council and at the three Pan-Orthodox Conferences in Rhodes (1961, 1963 and 1964).

Arriving at this kind of clarity required that long and intense process to which we shall refer subsequently and which is now known as the 'dialogue of charity'. In the phase immediately preceding the beginning of the dialogue, a specific study was undertaken by two commissions, one Catholic and one Orthodox, and finally a joint coordinating

* Mgr Fortino is Under-Secretary of the Pontifical Council for Promoting Christian Unity and Co-Secretary of the Joint International Commission for Theological Dialogue between the Roman Catholic and Orthodox Church.

committee was convened which agreed on a 'plan for getting underway the theological dialogue between the Roman Catholic Church and the Orthodox Church'. This joint preparatory document (JPD) constitutes the basis of the present phase of the dialogue in process.

I. Preparation and Planning of the Theological Dialogue

The opening of the theological dialogue was officially announced with the Common Declaration between the Ecumenical Patriarch Dimitrios I and Pope John Paul II which was made at the conclusion of the Pope's visit to the Phanar, on 30 November, 1979. In that Declaration, the decisive importance of the dialogue of charity for creating the necessary conditions for beginning theological conversations was underlined. Moreover, the dialogue of charity makes clear what are the indispensable conditions for the fruitful pursuit of the dialogue itself.

'The dialogue of charity (cf Jn 13:34; Eph 4:1-7), rooted in complete faithfulness to the one Lord Jesus Christ, and to his overriding will for his Church (cf Jn 17:21), has opened up the way to better understanding of our respective theological positions and thereby to new approaches to theological work and to a new attitude with regard to the common past of our Churches. The purification of the collective memory of our Churches is an important outcome of the dialogue of charity and an indispensable condition for future progress. The dialogue of charity itself must continue with might and main in the complex situation which we have inherited from the past, and which forms the real order of things in which our enterprise must be conducted today.'[1]

This slow recent process of spiritual preparation, which could be said to have its origin in the message of congratulations which Patriarch Athenagoras sent on the occasion of the election of Pope John XXIII in 1958, has had repercussions which have touched the conscience of Christians; at times, it has been truly prophetic in character.

Subsequent events, such as the meeting in 1964 between Paul VI and Athenagoras I in Jerusalem, the place where, 'to gather into one the scattered children of God' (Jn 11:52), our Lord Jesus Christ was 'raised up' on the cross; like the visit of Pope Paul VI to the Ecumenical Patriarch in 1967 and the visit to Rome of the Ecumenical Patriarch in 1967; like the visit to the Ecumenical Patriarchate in Constantinople by the new Pope John Paul II in 1979 and like the visit to Rome by the Patriarch of Antioch, Ignatius IV, in 1983; are only symbolic of a very wide-ranging new situation at various levels and in various fields which, if summarised, would still fail to do justice to all its aspects, to one or other of the two Churches or to the movement as a whole.[2] The very real difficulties that were confronted and overcome demonstrate the importance and the quality of a spiritual event which goes beyond the possibilities of human endeavour. The identifiable causes that can be adduced for this rapprochement include factors which range from a general political relaxation to the new bearings in relations between Rome and the East. These bearings include at least three elements: the reaffirmed ecclesial reality of the Orthodox Churches, together with the rediscovery of the theology of communion between sister Churches, a new psychological atmosphere of loyal ecclesial fraternity and the new methodology of dialogue in which the partners are placed on an equal footing. The doctrinal and spiritual contribution of the Second Vatican Council was decisive for securing the progress that has been made.[3]

While these developments in fraternal relations between the Churches were taking place, it was judged that the time was right for a 'technical preparation' of the theological dialogue which would directly have to confront doctrinal questions.

Patriarch Dimitrios I, in his message to Pope Paul VI on the occasion of the tenth anniversary of the abrogation of the reciprocal excommunications of 1054, on 7 December 1975, announced the Pan-Orthodox decision to create a commission to make a preparatory study. The Patriarch wrote that, in a sincere spirit of wanting to promote unity, 'we have made a synodal resolution to promote the holy cause of sacred ties with Rome and to move it onwards from the stage of the dialogue of charity to that of preparation for the theological dialogue'.

> 'With this in mind, after deliberations among the Orthodox Churches, we have reached the point where a Pan-Orthodox decision has been taken to set up a special inter-Orthodox technical theological commission to prepare the way from our side for this discussion.'[4]

The Catholic Church, for its part, did the same thing and set up its own preparatory commission. The commissions studied, in parallel, the planning of the theological dialogue. Subsequently, a joint coordinating committee finalised the above-mentioned joint document (JPD) which was then approved by both the Catholic and the Orthodox commissions.[5]

The JPD expressed the theological importance of the dialogue in three points: the *purpose* of the dialogue, the method and the theme for the first phase.

Having defined the purpose in the terms indicated at the beginning of this paper, the JPD deals with the question of method. 'The dialogue should begin with the elements that unite the Orthodox and Roman Catholic Churches' (II,1). This basic affirmation expressed the new methodology growing out of the new relationship and based on the dialogue of charity. It also drew together the conclusions of the long process of reflection that has been taking place in both Churches from the Council of Florence (1439) onwards. This method is to be distinguished from that used in theological conversations in the past which sought to affront 'differences' taken individually and in isolation from their theological and cultural contexts. Already in 1967, in his speech in St Peter's Basilica, addressed to Pope Paul VI, the Ecumenical Patriarch affirmed: 'As for the theological dialogue properly so-called, let us by common consent conduct this with a view, on the one hand, to the interpretation of what we both already live out in common in our Church life and, on the other, to the exploration of the truth in a spirit of charity and edification, and its formulation in a spirit of service.'[6] It is what is lived out in common by Catholics and Orthodox, not only in the past but also in the present, that constitutes in reality the solid basis for the dialogue. The process of interpretation referred to by Athenagoras draws attention both to legitimate diversity and to those questions which necessitate a real discussion to find a coherent solution for them on the basis of sacred Scripture and the great Tradition of the Church.

The JPD says:

'Regarding the themes which should be the object of the dialogue in its first stage, the study of the sacraments of the Church is judged favourably as facilitating an examination, in depth and in a positive way, of the problems of the dialogue' (III,1).

This proposal must be read in conjunction with the fundamental indication for the method of the dialogue that the same document proposes: 'The dialogue must begin with the elements that unite the Orthodox Church and the Roman Catholic Church.'

The study of the sacraments, moreover, is undertaken in the context of, and with the idea of beginning with, a solid datum which is common to both Churches: sacramental reality, a reality that stands beyond every theological, liturgical and disciplinary consideration; and, above all, an objective reality which remains so independently of all subjective speculation.

The JPD gives the reason for this choice and outlines the implicit problem.

'Sacramental experience and theology express themselves through one another. For this reason, the study of the sacraments of the Church presents itself as a very positive and natural theme. From the study of the problems related to the sacraments, one will normally come to an examination of the ecclesiological aspects as well as other aspects of the faith, without moving away from the lived character which is fundamental to theology' (III,1).

A choice is effectively made, therefore, to consider the nature of the Church, and consequently its unity.

For the purpose of reestablishing full communion between the Catholic Church and the Orthodox Churches, the study of the sacraments is a 'very positive' theme, because the sacraments are common to the two Churches, and 'natural' in the sense that they are part of the nature of the Church as the sacrament of salvation. It is asserted, moreover, that 'the lived character' that is the life of the Church is fundamental for theology.

Consequently and accordingly, the JPD gives methodological indications, both (1.) about the meaning of the assertion that the dialogue must begin with the elements that unite the Churches, as well as (2.) on the connection between the study of the sacraments and the search for unity, a search which will have to confront and resolve the existing divergences between Catholics and Orthodox. We shall consider these two factors in turn.

1. Beginning with the elements that unite 'in no way means that it is desirable, or even possible, to avoid the problems which still divide the two Churches'.

'It only means that the beginning of the dialogue should be made in a positive spirit and that this spirit should prevail when treating the problems which have accumulated during a separation lasting many centuries' (II,1).

It is necessary, therefore, to take into consideration 'more recent developments, both of a theological and of an ecclesial nature, in the relations between the two Churches', and that both in the Catholic Church and in the Orthodox Churches. 'In the light of these, the points of difference between our Churches can also be considered in a new way' (II,2). To do this in a fruitful way for the theme of the sacraments, the JPD maintains that 'the dialogue commission must free itself as far as possible from the problems created in the past by scholastic theology'.

The document is a joint one, and this last assertion refers at the same time and in the same degree to a particular manualistic theology of the schools that is to be found both in the Catholic Church and in the Orthodox Church. Consequently and explicitly, the JPD maintains that one must take account 'seriously of all recent theological endeavours'.

But the Catholic-Orthodox theological dialogue does not have the task of preparing a new manual of sacramental theology. The principal purpose of the study of the sacraments is not to examine all the aspects of the theme, 'but in the first place the aspects which touch on the unity of the Church. Consequently, the principal problems that must be proposed for discussion are linked to ecclesiology in its broadest sense' (III,3).

Within the framework of this broad theme, the JPD makes a theological planning option to make the research more coherent. In this plan, eucharistic ecclesiology has a privileged place.

'If one tries to connect the problematic regarding sacraments to the tradition of the early Church, one will see that, in principle and in essence, when there is a question of many sacraments, these are conceived as expressing one sacrament, the "Sacrament of Christ", which expresses itself and is realised by the Holy Spirit as the Sacrament of the Church. The sacraments should not be conceived of principally as autonomous actions or as individualistic means of the transmission of divine grace, but as the expression and realisation of the unique sacrament of the Church.' (III,4)

It goes on:

'This unique sacrament of the Church is expressed and realised in history above all in the Holy Eucharist.... The Eucharist, then, should not be considered as one sacrament among others, but as the sacrament *par excellence* of the Church. Consequently, it should be the basis of every examination of the theme of the sacraments within the framework of the dialogue' (III,5).

2. But what is the connection between the study of the sacraments and the search for the unity of the Church?

The JPD, referring to the first phase of the dialogue, does not go into all the outstanding problems facing Catholics and Orthodox, but effectively opens the dialogue to all the wider problems. And all the proposals are put forward 'on this basis and with this point of departure: the sacrament of the Holy Eucharist'. As can be seen, the JPD considers the Eucharist as the sacrament *par excellence* of the Church, and the common celebration of the Eucharist as the expression of the reestablishment of full unity. The document asks, moreover, that the commission should study in its first phase several fundamental problems. In order to indicate the perceived connection between sacraments and the search for unity, I mention some of these:

a) 'In what sense is right faith (orthodoxy) related to the sacraments of the Church?' (III,6,d). This question addresses the problem of the relationship between faith and the sacraments, the question of the right profession of faith, of *communicatio in sacris*, and of whether or not partial intercommunion is possible. In particular, between Catholics and Orthodox, are there (and, if so, what are they?) divergences of faith which prevent a common celebration of the sacraments?

b) 'Granted that the Church builds itself up and is realised in time and space by the Eucharist of the local community gathered around one sole bishop, what does this fact mean for the communion of all the local churches and their witness to the world?' (III,6,c)

Here we find posited the problem of the relationship between the local church and the universal Church, collegiality, and the role of the Bishop of Rome in the communion of the various local churches.

c) 'What is the relationship of the sacraments – always conceived of as connected with the Holy Eucharist – with the structure and government of the Church (or the canonical unity of the Church)?' (III,6,b)

Here is posited, among other things, the question of the relationship between sacrament and canonical jurisdiction, between sacraments and canon law, and a range of problems which refer directly to the unity of the Church.

d) Moreover:

'How should the entire structure and the realisation of the sacramental life of the Church be understood in relationship to Christ and in relationship to the Holy Spirit? What relation exists between sacraments and Christology, pneumatology and triadology?' (III,7,a)

It is in this optic that questions concerning, for example, the epiclesis of the Holy Spirit or the empirical elements of the sacrament, or even the relationship of the celebrant and of the community to Christ and the Holy Spirit, as well as the question of the *filioque*, must be situated.

e) In addition, what is the internal relationship of the sacraments to the Eucharist; in particular, 'what is the relation of the other "sacraments of initiation", that is, Baptism and Chrismation/Confirmation, to the Holy Eucharist?' Given that practice is different in East and West, 'what importance does this question have for the concept of the unity of the Church and even for the spiritual life of the faithful?' (III,6,a)

f) 'There should also be attached to this the problem of the sense of eschatology in the understanding of the sacraments.' (III,7,b)

g) 'Finally, the anthropological question, which has different accentuations in the East and in the West, should not be overlooked in studying the sacraments' (III,7,c). What is the new creation brought about in humanity by the sacraments and what is its influence on the transformation of society and on the natural and cosmic order?

Here what is being proposed is the whole relationship between the Church and the world.

These quotations have sought to indicate the general orientations that have been proposed for the dialogue between Catholics and Orthodox with the sacraments as their basis. What we have here is an organic vision which corresponds to the sacramental nature of the Church.

II. The Development of the Theological Dialogue

The JPD was approved by the authorities both of the Catholic Church and of the fourteen Orthodox

Churches.[7] It is important to note, therefore, that it constitutes much more than simply a programme of study.

Once the joint commission had been appointed (56 members: 28 Orthodox and 28 Catholics) and publicised on the occasion of the visit of Pope John Paul II to the Ecumenical Patriarchate,[8] the official theological conversations could begin as a bilateral dialogue. That happened in 1980 and, to date, the commission has held six plenary meetings.

1. Patmos/Rhodes, 28 May to 4 June, 1980.
2. Munich, 30 June to 6 July, 1982.
3. Crete, 30 May to 8 June, 1984.
4. Bari, 28 May to 7 June, 1986
   and 9 to 16 June, 1987.
5. Uusi Valamo, 19 to 27 June, 1988.
6. Freising, 6 to 15 June, 1990.

In its first session, the joint commission approved the plan for the dialogue (JPD) as an agenda for the first phase of the dialogue, and established some practical arrangements for procedure. It set up three joint subcommissions that would study the same question in parallel. Furthermore, a coordinating committee would work out an organic synthesis to submit to the plenary session for its study, re-elaboration and approval. The plenary meeting would take place, in principle, every two years. In between plenary sessions, the subcommissions would meet.

III. The Three Published Documents

Up to date, the joint commission has published three documents which are intimately related with one another.

1. 'The Mystery of the Church and of the Eucharist in the Light of the Mystery of the Holy Trinity' (1982).

2. 'Faith, Sacraments and the Unity of the Church' (1987).

3. 'The Sacrament of Order in the Sacramental Structure of the Church, with particular reference to the importance of Apostolic Succession for the Sanctification and Unity of the People of God' (1988).

In the first document, the members of the commission state that they are dealing with 'the mystery of the Church in only one of its aspects' which, 'however, is particularly important in the sacramental perspective of the Church'. Moreover, they state that 'we intend to show that in doing so we are expressing together a faith which is the continuation of that of the apostles' (Introduction). These two indications give the exact perspective in which the affirmations of the document should be read. The members of the commission situate themselves together in the line of the apostolic faith and express substantially a common sacramental conception of the Church. This is done through the development of a eucharistic ecclesiology which the document sets out in three points: a) the relationship between the Eucharist and the Church, b) the Eucharist in local churches around the bishop, and c) the local church and the universal Church.

The document, in speaking of the functions of bishops in local churches and in the universal Church, opens up the question of 'conciliar practice' in the life of the Church.

'The presence of bishops from neighbouring sees at [a bishop's] episcopal ordination 'sacramentalises' and actualises [the] *communion* [between bishops].

It produces a thorough fusion between his solicitude for the local community and care for the Church spread throughout the world. The *episkope* of the universal Church is entrusted by the Spirit to the totality of local bishops in *communion* with one another. This *communion* is expressed traditionally in conciliar practice. We shall have to examine further the way in which the latter is conceived and realised in the perspective of what we have just explained' (III,4).

From the Munich document we get the image of the *koinonia* which should characterise the unity of the churches: *'communion* in faith, hope and love, *communion* in the sacraments, *communion* in the diversity of charisms, *communion* in reconciliation and *communion* in ministry' (III,4). Up to this point, Catholics and Orthodox are expressing a common conception of the Church. But, in this context and in this perspective, there still remains to be analysed the question of the role of the Bishop of Rome in the Church of Christ.

In the second document, the relationship between 'Faith, Sacraments and the Unity of the Church' was addressed. The document can be summarised in three affirmations which assist an understanding of the text as a whole.

a. The profession of faith and the celebration of the sacraments: 'Every sacrament presupposes and expresses the faith of the Church which celebrates it' (I,6).

b. Common faith and concelebration of the sacraments: identity of faith is necessary for concelebration of the sacraments. This is possible only between members of churches who have a common faith, the priesthood and the sacraments: communion in faith and communion in the sacraments are not two distinct realities. '[C]ommunion in the sacraments expresses the identity and unicity of the true faith which the churches share' (I,23). And it is through reciprocal recognition of the identity and unicity of faith, as also of priesthood and the sacraments, which are transmitted in each of the local churches, that they can recognise one another as churches of God, and that each member of the faithful is accepted by the churches as a brother or sister in faith and can participate in the sacraments.

c. Unicity of faith and variety of expression: 'However, a certain diversity in [the] formulation [of faith] does not compromise the *koinonia* between local churches when each church can recognise, under the variety of formulations, the one authentic faith received from the apostles' (I,25). In the first millennium, when Christians of East and West lived in full communion, the variety of creeds and theological expressions of the common faith created no danger for sacramental communion. A good example of this can be the profession of faith used in the celebration of Baptism. While, in the East, the creed of Nicea-Constantinople was regularly used, in the churches of the West use was made of what is known as the Apostles' Creed. The affirmation of the principle of 'unity in diversity' is essential for the organic reestablishment of communion between East and West. In this perspective, we find consideration of the sacraments of Christian initiation in the West which, in the course of the centuries, has taken on a different pastoral practice from the East (the separation in time of the three sacraments of Baptism, Confirmation and the Eucharist and, subsequently, the practice of receiving the Eucharist before Confirmation).

The document left this question open and recalled the doctrinal presuppositions of pastoral practice.

'This inversion, which provokes objections or understandable reservations among both Orthodox and Roman Catholics, calls for deep theological and pastoral reflection because pastoral practice should never lose sight of the meaning of the early tradition and its doctrinal importance' (II,51).

The third document dealt with the problems of the sacrament of Order and apostolic succession. It is a particularly important topic in the context of the conception – common to Orthodox and Roman Catholics – of the sacramental structure of the Church and of the communion of bishops, who are successors of the apostles. The bishops are guarantors of the unity of the individual particular churches and of the communion of these churches which is expressed in conciliar practice. This is a reality both at the local level (local councils) and at the level of the universal Church (ecumenical councils). This document, like the previous one, opens up the perspective in which the question of the role of the bishop of Rome in the Church must be studied.

'It is in this perspective of communion among local churches that an approach could be made to the question of primacy in the Church in general and, in particular, to that of the primacy of the bishop of Rome, which constitutes a serious divergence between us and which will be discussed in the future' (IV,55).

In the common declaration between the Ecumenical Patriarch Dimitrios I and Pope John Paul II which concluded the Patriarch's visit to Rome, on 7 December 1987, we find a positive appreciation of the two documents which had been published at that time. In that appreciation, one can logically include the third document as well. The Pope and the Patriarch declared:

'We express our joy and satisfaction in taking note of the first results and the positive evolution of the theological dialogue announced at the time of our meeting at the Phanar on 30 November, 1979. The documents accepted by the mixed commission constitute important points of reference for the continuation of the dialogue. Indeed, they seek to express what the Catholic Church and the Orthodox Church can already profess together as their common faith regarding the mystery of the Church and the bond between faith and the sacraments. Since each of our Churches has received and celebrates the same sacraments, they perceive better that, when unity in faith is assured, a certain diversity of expression, often complementary, and of proper usages, does not create an obstacle but enriches the life of the Church and the understanding, always imperfect, of the muystery revealed (cf 1Cor 13:12).[9]

IV. Discussions in Progress and Perspectives

The dialogue has been pursued slowly but with sure progress along the path undertaken. It was on the point of producing another document of undoubted importance. The subcommissions and the coordinating committee had prepared a draft document on 'The Ecclesiological and Canonical Consequences of the Sacramental Structure of the Church: Conciliarity and

Authority in the Church'. But in the plenary session of Freising (6 to 15 June, 1990), at the request of the Orthodox, another problem was addressed which, however, was already a preoccupation of the commission and which the commission had already set up a special subcommission to examine.

The *communiqué* approved at the conclusion of the 1990 session affirms: 'Because of recent events, the whole session was devoted to study of the questions posed by the origin, existence and development of the Catholic Churches of the Byzantine rite.' Recent developments (1989: the fall of communist regimes and the reestablishment of the principle of religious liberty) have made possible the reorganisation of the Byzantine Catholic Churches in the Ukraine and Romania with consequent tension with the Orthodox, especially in regard to the question of the ownership of places of worship which, in 1946 and 1948, were confiscated by the respective communist governments and given in part to the Orthodox Church. Under the pressure of these events and of the strong feelings which they provoked, the commission made an initial study of the issues, concluding that they needed to be studied further at the next session.[10]

Consequently, the subcommissions have examined its important aspects and the coordinating committee, which met in Ariccia from 10 to 15 June, 1991, has prepared a draft document on 'Uniatism, Former Method of Union, and the Present Search for Full Communion'. The *communiqué* published at the end of the meeting of the coordinating committee in Ariccia said the following:

'The document prepared at Ariccia will be examined at the next plenary session of the commission which is planned for 17 to 26 June, 1992. The document is made up of two parts. In the first part, an attempt is made to describe the elements of the situation in question. In the second, suggestions are offered both to the faithful of the two Churches and to their leaders.The document is based on the ecclesiological shifts which occurred at the Pan-Orthodox Conferences and at the Second Vatican Council. Indeed, we have moved from a situation in which each Church claims to be the only means of salvation to the conviction that the two are sister Churches. This shift opened the way for a dialogue of charity, truth and sincerity.'[11]

Moreover, a faithful clarification of this topic, without the passions inherited from the past but with the crucial help of history, and in the light of the new spiritual and theological indications provided by modern ecumenical research, could render an authentic service to relations between Catholics and Orthodox, as also to the life of the Eastern Catholic Churches themselves.

To facilitate the solution to this question, John Paul II has written a letter to the bishops of Europe: 'On Relations between Catholics and Orthodox in the New Situation of Central and Eastern Europe'. The letter concludes with these words:

'It is my heartfelt hope that wherever Oriental Catholics and Orthodox live side by side there will be established relations which are fraternal, mutually respectful and sincerely seeking a common testimony to the one Lord. This will help not only coexistence in practical circumstances but will also facilitate the theological dialogue directed to over-

coming whatever still divides Catholics and Orthodox. Being faithful witnesses to Jesus Christ who
has set us free should be the main concern in our
time of cultural, social and political changes, so
that we can preach together and with credibility the
one Gospel of salvation, and be builders of peace
and reconciliation in a world always threatened by
conflicts and wars.'[12]

This will obviously substantially facilitate the taking up again of the theological discussion and the
addressing of the major questions that still have to be
confronted on the path to full communion between the
Catholic Church and the Orthodox Churches.

NOTES

1. E.J.Stormon, SJ, *Towards the Healing of Schism: The Sees of Rome and
Constantinople* (Paulist Press, New York, 1987), pp. 367-368.
2. Cf Eleuterio F.Fortino, 'Il dialogo tra Cattolici e Ortodossi. Panoramica
e prospettive', in *La chiesa cattolica oggi nel dialogo – Corso breve
d'ecumenismo*, Vol. 4 (Centro Pro Unione, Roma, 1982), pp. 7-17. A
synthetic account of the major events is given there. These positive
developments were recorded and publicised in Church documentation,
especially in the journals which are particularly interested in the Christian East, such as *Istina* (Paris), *Irénikon* (Chevetogne, Belgium), *Proche
Orient Chrétien* (Jerusalem) and *Oriente Cristiano* (Palermo). From
1967 onwards, precise information is found in the *Information Service*
of the Secretariat for Promoting Christian Unity.
3. Eleuterio F.Fortino, 'Le relazioni con le chiese orientali a venti anni dal
Decreto sull'Ecumenismo', *Studi Ecumenici* 2(1984), pp. 517-538.
4. Stormon, *Towards the Healing of Schism*, p. 280.
5. The entire technical preparation took place in the following phases:
a) 14 December, 1975: tenth anniversary of the abrogation of the
excommunications between Rome and Constantinople. On this occasion, in two parallel ceremonies at Rome and at the Phanar, the Ecumenical Patriarch and the Pope announced the decision to set up two
commissions, one Catholic and one Pan-Orthodox, for the preparation
of theological dialogue with the Orthodox Church and the Catholic
Church, respectively.

b) 11 to 15 October, 1976: first meeting of the Catholic commission for the preparation of theological dialogue with the Orthodox Church. Members of the commission: Rev Fr Pierre Duprey, Rev Fr Miguel Arranz, SJ, Rev Fr Carmelo Capizzi, SJ, Rev Fr Christophe Dumont, OP, Rev Dom Emmanuel Lanne, OSB, Rev Fr John Long, SJ, Rev Fr Pierre Mouallem, Rev Fr Peter Sheehan, Rev Mgr Eleuterio Fortino (Secretary). In its report, the commission formulated suggestions about the spirit in which the dialogue should be planned from the Catholic point of view and on the method to follow and the themes to address.

c) June, 1977: first meeting of the inter-Orthodox technical theological commission for dialogue with the Catholic Church. The commission produced a document on the purpose of the dialogue, its methodology and its themes. The commission proposed the setting up of a working group for coordination.

'The present technical commission of theologians is of the opinion that as part of the work of the two commissions – the Roman Catholic one and the Orthodox one – there needs to be set up by common consent a small working group for their coordination, which will help to direct the work of the two commissions towards the realisation of the future dialogue in a way that is constructive for unity.'

d) 14 to 28 November, 1977: second meeting of the inter-Orthodox technical theological commission. The commission 'devoted its second session to the study of the manner of approach to the theme of the sacraments which has been judged the most auspicious theme for the inauguration of the dialogue'.

e) The two documents produced by the Orthodox commission were communicated to the Catholic commission. The Metropolitan of Carthage, Parthenios, Co-President of the Coordinating Committee, after the first meetings of both the commissions, made the following comment. 'Both commissions are working very attentively in accordance with the ancient adage, "*festina lente*", because they are convinced that on this depends the whole history of both of these two ancient and principal Churches' (*L'Osservatore Romano*, 24 March 1978).

f) 29 March to 1 April, 1978: meeting of the Coordinating Committee. After their setting up in 1976, the two commissions carried out their preparatory work within each of the respective Churches. By common agreement, they formed a coordinating group to examine together the work already done on both sides. The coordinating group was composed, on the Orthodox side, of: Metropolitan Parthenios of Carthage (President), Archbishop Kyrill of Vyborg, Rev Prof Ion Bria, Prof John Zizioulas, Archimandrite Spyridon Papageorgiou (Secretary). On the Catholic side: Bishop Ramon Torrella (President), Rev Pierre Duprey, Rev Fr John Lang, SJ, Rev Dom Emmanuel Lanne, OSB, Rev Mgr Eleuterio Fortino (Secretary). In the course of the meeting, the coordinating group considered the aim of the dialogue, the method to follow in the dialogue and the themes to be considered in its first phase. The group agreed on a plan of action that would be submitted to the two responsible commissions for their consideration and for eventual presentation to the authorities of the two Churches. When the preparatory work was finished, the authorities of the Catholic Church and of the Orthodox Church would be in a position to take concrete decisions about the formal opening of a theological dialogue between the Catholic Church and the Orthodox Church.

g) 8 to 10 May, 1978: second meeting of the Catholic commission for the preparation of the dialogue with the Orthodox Church. The commission examined the document produced by the Coordinating Committee. It approved it substantially, while making some amendments.

h) 25 to 27 June, 1978. Third meeting of the inter-Orthodox technical commission. The commission examined the document produced by the Coordinating Committee together with the amendments proposed by the Catholic commission. The commission approved the document and welcomed almost all of the amendments proposed by the Catholic commission.

i) By correspondence, the Co-Presidents of the Coordinating Committee definitively agreed on the final text and submitted it to the respective authorities as the result of all the preparatory work that had taken place.

6. Stormon, *Towards the Healing of Schism*, p. 173.
7. The fourteen Orthodox Churches involved in the dialogue are the *patriarchates* (Constantinople, Alexandria, Antioch, Jerusalem, Moscow, Serbia, Romania and Bulgaria) and the *autocephalous Churches* (Cyprus, Greece, Poland, Georgia, Czechoslovakia), as well as the autonomous Church of Finland.
8. SPCU, *Information Service*, n.41, 1979(IV), pp. 17-34.
9. SPCU, *Information Service*, n.66, 1988(I), p. 29.
10. PCPCU, *Information Service*, n.73, 1990(II), pp. 52-53.
11. *L'Osservatore Romano* (English edition), 1 July, 1991, p. 3.
12. Pope John Paul's letter is reproduced in full as an Appendix in this volume.

The Mystery of the Church
and of the Eucharist in the Light
of the Mystery of the Holy Trinity
*(Munich, 1982)**

Introduction

Faithful to the mandate received at Rhodes, this report touches upon the mystery of the Church in only one of its aspects. This aspect, however, is particularly important in the sacramental perspective of the Church, that is, the mystery of the Church and of the Eucharist in the light of the mystery of the Holy Trinity. As a matter of fact, the request was made to start with what we have in common and, by developing it, to tackle from within and progressively all the points on which we are not in agreement.

In composing this document, we intend to show that in doing so we are expressing together a faith which is the continuation of that of the apostles.

This document marks the first step in the effort to fulfil the programme of the preparatory commission, approved at the first meeting of the commission for dialogue.

Since it is a question of a first step, touching upon the mystery of the Church inonly one of its aspects, many points are not yet treated here. They will be treated in succeeding steps as has been foreseen in the programme mentioned above.

---

* This first agreed statement was finalised at the second plenary meeting of the international dialogue, held from 30 June to 6 July, 1982, at the Fürstenried retreat centre, Munich, Germany.

I. The Ministry of Christ

(1) Christ, the Son of God incarnate, dead and risen, is the only one who has conquered sin and death. To speak, therefore, of the sacramental nature of the mystery of Christ is to evoke the possibility given to man and, through him, to the whole cosmos, to experience the new creation, the Kingdom of God, here and now, through material and created realities. This is the mode (*tropos*) in which the unique person and the unique event of Christ exist and operate in history from Pentecost until the Parousia. However, the eternal life which God has given to the world in the event of Christ, His eternal Son, is contained in earthen vessels. As yet, it is given only as a foretaste, as a pledge.

(2) At the Last Supper, Christ stated that he was giving his Body to the disciples for the life of the many, in the Eucharist. This gift is given there by God to the world, but in sacramental form. From that moment, the Eucharist exists as the sacrament of Christ himself. It becomes the foretaste of eternal life, the medicine of immortality, the sign of the Kingdom to come. The sacrament of the Christ-event thus passes into the sacrament of the Eucharist, the sacrament which incorporates us fully into Christ.

(3) The incarnation of the Son of God, his death and resurrection were realised from the beginning, according to the will of the Father, in the Holy Spirit. This Spirit, who proceeds eternally from the Father and manifests himself through the Son, prepared the Christ-event and realised it fully in the resurrection. Christ, who is the Sacrament *par excellence*, given by the Father for the world, continues to give himself for the many in the Spirit, who alone gives life (Jn 6). The

sacrament of Christ is also a reality which can exist
only in the Spirit.

The Church and the Eucharist

(4a) Although, in the account of the Last Supper,
the evangelists are silent about the action of the Spirit,
he was nonetheless united more than ever to the incarnate Son for the fulfilment of the Father's work. He is
not yet given, received as a Person, by the disciples
(Jn 7:39). But, when Jesus is glorified, then the Spirit
himself also pours himself out and manifests himself.
The Lord Jesus enters into the glory of the Father and,
at the same time, by the outpouring of the Spirit, into
his sacramental *tropos* in this world. Pentecost, the
completion of the paschal mystery, inaugurates simultaneously the last times. The Eucharist and the Church,
Body of the crucified and risen Christ, become the
place of the energies of the Holy Spirit.

b) Believers are baptised in the Spirit in the name
of the Holy Trinity to form one body (cf 1 Cor 12:13).
When the Church celebrates the Eucharist, it realises
'what it is', the Body of Christ (1 Cor 10:17). By
Baptism and Chrismation (Confirmation), the members of Christ are actually anointed by the Spirit, grafted
into Christ. But, by the Eucharist, the paschal event
opens itself out into the Church. The Church becomes
what it is called to be by Baptism and Chrismation. By
communion in the Body and Blood of Christ, the
faithful grow in that mystical divinisation which makes
them dwell in the Son and in the Father, through the
Spirit.

c) Thus, on the one hand, the Church celebrates the
Eucharist as the expression here and now of the heav-

enly liturgy; but, on the other hand, the Eucharist builds up the Church in the sense that, through it, the Spirit of the risen Christ fashions the Church into the Body of Christ. That is why the Eucharist is truly the Sacrament of the Church, both as sacrament of the total gift the Lord makes of himself to his own and as manifestation and growth of the Body of Christ, the Church. The pilgrim Church celebrates the Eucharist on earth until its Lord comes to restore kingshipto God the Father so that God may be all in all. It thus anticipates the judgement of the world and its final transfiguration.

The mission of the Spirit

(5)   The mission of the Spirit remains joined to that of the Son. The celebration of the Eucharist reveals the divine energies manifested by the Spirit at work in the Body of Christ.

a) The Spirit *prepares* the coming of Christ by announcing it through the prophets, by directing the history of the chosen people towards him, by causing him to be conceived by the Virgin Mary and by opening up hearts to his word.

b) The Spirit *manifests* Christ in his work as Saviour, the Gospel which he himself is. The eucharistic celebration is the *anamnesis* (the memorial): truly, but sacramentally, today, the *ephapax* [the once and for all] is and becomes present. The celebration of the Eucharist is *par excellence* the *kairos* [proper time] of the mystery.

c) The Spirit *transforms* the sacred gifts into the Body and Blood of Christ (*metabole*) in order to bring about the growth of the Body which is the Church. In this sense the entire celebration is an *epiclesis* [invocation], which becomes more explicit at certain moments. The Church is continually in a state of *epiclesis*.

d) The Spirit *puts into communion* with the Body of Christ those who share the same bread and the same cup. Starting from there, the Church manifests what it is, the sacrament of the Trinitarian *koinonia* [communion], the 'dwelling of God with men' (cf Rev 21:4).

By making present what Christ did once and for all – the event of the mystery – the Spirit accomplishes it in all of us. This relation to the mystery, more evident in the Eucharist, is found in the other sacraments, all acts of the Spirit. That is why the Eucharist is the centre of sacramental life.

(6) Taken as a whole, the eucharistic celebration makes present the Trinitarian mystery of the Church. In it, one passes from hearing the Word, culminating in the proclamation of the Gospel, the apostolic announcing of the Word made flesh, to the thanksgiving offered to the Father, to the memorial of the sacrifice of Christ and to communion in him thanks to the prayer of *epiclesis* uttered in faith. For, in the Eucharist, the *epiclesis* is not merely an invocation for the sacramental transforming of the bread and of the cup. It is also a prayer for the full effect of the communion of all in the mystery revealed by the Son.

In this way, the presence of the Spirit himself extends, by the sharing in the sacrament of the Word made flesh, to the whole body of the Church. Without wishing to resolve yet the difficulties which have arisen between the East and the West concerning the relationship between the Son and the Spirit, we can already say together that this Spirit, who proceeds from the Father (Jn 15:26) as from the sole source in the Trinity, and who has become the Spirit of our sonship

41

(Rom 8:15) since he is also the Spirit of the Son (Gal 4:6), is communicated to us particularly in the Eucharist by this Son upon whom he reposes in time and in eternity (Jn 1:32).

That is why the eucharistic mystery is accomplished in the prayer which joins together the words by which the Word made flesh instituted the sacrament and the *epiclesis* in which the Church, moved by faith, entreats the Father, through the Son, to send the Spirit so that, in the unique offering of the incarnate Son, everything may be consummated in unity. Through the Eucharist, believers unite themselves to Christ, who offers himself to the Father with them, and they receive the possibility of offering themselves in a spirit of sacrifice to each other, as Christ himself offered himself to the Father for the many, thus giving himself to men.

This consummation in unity, brought about by the one inseparable operation of the Son and the Spirit, acting in reference to the Father and to His design, is the Church in its fulness.

II. The Mystery of God, One in Three Persons

(1) If one looks at the New Testament, one will notice first of all that the Church designates a 'local' reality. The Church exists in history as [the] local church. For a region, one speaks more often of churches, in the plural. It is always a question of the Church of God, but in a given place.

Now the Church existing in a given place is not formed, in a radical sense, by the persons who come together to establish it. There is a 'Jerusalem from on high' which 'comes down from God', a communion which is the foundation of the community itself. The Church comes into being by a free gift, that of the new creation.

However, it is clear that the Church 'which is in' a given place manifests itself as such when it is 'assembled'. This assembly itself, whose elements and requirements are indicated by the New Testament, is fully such when it is the eucharistic *synaxis* [assembly]. When the local church celebrates the Eucharist, the event which took place 'once and for all' is actually made present and manifested. In the local church, then, there is neither male nor female, slave nor free, Jew nor Greek. A new unity is communicated which overcomes divisions and restores communion in the one Body of Christ. This unity transcends psychological, racial, socio-political or cultural unity. It is the 'communion of the Holy Spirit' gathering together the scattered children of God. The newness of Baptism and of Chrismation then bears its fruit. And, by the power of the Body and Blood of the Lord, filled with the Holy Spirit, there is healed that sin which does not cease to assail Christians, raising obstacles to the dynamism of the 'life for God in Christ Jesus' received in Baptism. This applies also to the sin of division, all of whose forms contradict God's design.

One of the chief texts to remember is 1Cor 10:15-17: one Bread, one Cup, one Body of Christ in the plurality of members. This mystery of the unity in love of many persons constitutes the real newness of the Trinitarian *koinonia* communicated to men in the Church through the Eucharist. Such is the purpose of Christ's saving work, which is spread abroad in the last times, from Pentecost onwards.

That is why the Church finds its model, its origin and its end in the mystery of God, one in three Persons. Further still, the Eucharist thus understood in the light of the Trinitarian mystery is the criterion for the functioning of the life of the Church as a whole. The institutional elements should be nothing but a visible reflection of the reality of the mystery.

(2) The unfolding of the eucharistic celebration of the local church shows how *koinonia* takes shape in the church celebrating the Eucharist. In the Eucharist celebrated by the local church actively gathered around the bishop, or the priest in communion with him, the following aspects stand out, interconnected among themselves, even if this or that moment of the celebration emphasises one or another aspect.

Koinonia is eschatological. It is the newness which comes in the last times. That is why everything in the Eucharist, as in the life of the Church, begins with conversion and reconciliation. The Eucharist presupposes repentance (*metanoia*) and confession (*exomologesis*), which find in other circumstances their own sacramental expression. But the Eucharist forgives and heals sins also, since it is the sacrament of the divinising love of the Father, by the Son, in the Holy Spirit.

But this *koinonia* is also kerygmatic. This is evident in the *synaxis* not only because the celebration 'announces' the event of the mystery, but also because it actualises it today in the Spirit. This implies the proclamation of the Word to the assembly and the response of faith given by all. Thus comes about the communion of the assembly in the kerygma, and hence unity in faith. Orthodoxy [correct faith] is inherent in the eucharistic *koinonia*. This orthodoxy is expressed most clearly through the proclamation of the symbol of faith [the Creed] which is a summary of the apostolic tradition of which the bishop is the witness in virtue of his succession. Thus, the Eucharist is inseparably Sacrament and Word since in it the incarnate Word sanctifies in the Spirit. That is why the entire liturgy, and not only the reading of the Holy Scriptures, constitutes a proclamation of the Word under the form of doxology and prayer. On the other hand, the word proclaimed is the Word made flesh and become sacramental.

Koinonia is both ministerial and pneumatological. That is why the Eucharist is its manifestation *par excellence*. The entire assembly, each one in his place, is *leitourgos* [minister] of the koinonia and is such only by the Holy Spirit. While being a gift of the Trinitarian God, *koinonia* is also the response of men. In the faith which comes from the Spirit and from the Word, they put into practice the vocation and the mission received in Baptism: to become, each in his place, living members of the Body of Christ.

The ministry of the bishop

(3) The ministry of the bishop is not merely a tactical or pragmatic function (because a president is necessary) but an organic function. The bishop receives the gift of episcopal grace (1Tim 4:14) in the sacrament of consecration effected by bishops who themselves have received this gift, thanks to the existence of an uninterrupted series of episcopal ordinations, beginning from the holy apostles. By the sacrament of ordination, the Spirit of the Lord 'confers' on the bishop, not juridically, as if it were a pure transmission of power, but sacramentally, the *exousia* [authority] of Servant which the Son received from the Father and which he assumed in a human way by his acceptance of his passion.

The function of the bishop is closely bound to the eucharistic assembly over which he presides. The eucharistic unity of the local church implies communion between the one who presides and the people to whom he delivers the Word of Salvation and the eucharistic gifts. Furthermore, the minister is also the one who 'receives' from his church, which is faithful to tradition, this word which he transmits. And the great intercession which he sends up to the Father is simply that of his entire church with him. The bishop cannot be separated from his church any more than a church can be separated from its bishop.

The bishop stands at the heart of the local church as minister of the Spirit to discern charisms and take care that they are exercised in harmony, for the good of all, in faithfulness to the apostolic tradition. He puts himself at the service of the initiatives of the Spirit so that nothing may prevent them from contributing to building up *koinonia*. He is minister of unity, servant of Christ the Lord, whose mission is to 'gather into unity the children of God'. And because the Church is built up by the Eucharist, it is he, invested with the grace of priestly ministry, who presides at the latter.

But this presidency must be properly understood. The bishop presides at the offering which is that of his entire community. By consecrating the gifts so that they become the Body and Blood the community offers, he celebrates not only for it, nor only with it and in it, but through it. He appears then as minister of Christ fashioning the unity of his Body, creating *communion* through his body. The union of the community with him is first of all of the order of *mysterion* [mystery] and not primordially of the juridical order. It is that union expressed in the Eucharist which is prolonged and given practical expression in the 'pastoral' relations of teaching, government and sacramental life. The ecclesial community is thus called to be the outline of a human community renewed.

(4) There is profound *communion* between the bishop and the community in which the Spirit gives him responsibility for the Church of God. The ancient tradition expressed it happily in the image of marriage. But this communion is located in the context of communion with the apostolic community. In the ancient tradition (as the Apostolic Tradition of Hippolytus notably proves) the bishop elected by the people – who guarantee his apostolic faith, in conformity with what the local church confesses – receives the ministerial grace of Christ by the Spirit in the prayer of the assembly and by the laying on of hands (*chirotonia*) of the neighbouring bishops, witnesses of the faith of their own churches. His charism, coming directly from the Spirit, is given to him in the apostolicity of his church (linked to the faith of the apostolic community) and in that of the other churches represented by their bishop. His ministry is thereby inserted into the catholicity of the Church of God.

Apostolic succession, therefore, means something more than a mere transmission of powers. It is succession in a church which witnesses to the apostolic faith, in *communion* with the other churches which witness to the same apostolic faith. The see (*cathedra*) plays an essential role in inserting the bishop into the heart of ecclesial apostolicity. On the other hand, once ordained, the bishop becomes in his church the guarantor of apostolicity, the one who represents it within the *communion* of churches and its link with other churches. That is why, in his church, any Eucharist can be celebrated *in truth* only if presided over by him or by a presbyter *in communion* with him. Mention of him in the *anaphora* [eucharistic prayer] is essential.

Through the ministry of presbyters, charged with presiding over the life and the eucharistic celebration of the communities entrusted to them, these communities grow in *communion* with all the communities for which the bishop has primary responsibility. In the present situation, the diocese itself is a *communion* of eucharistic communities. One of the essential functions of presbyters is to link these to the Eucharist of the bishop and to nourish them with the apostolic faith of which the bishop is the witness and guarantor. They should also take care that Christians, nourished by the Body and Blood of him who gave his life for his brethren, should be authentic witnesses of fraternal love in the reciprocal sacrifice nourished by the sacrifice of Christ. For, according to the saying of the apostle, 'if someone sees his brother in need and closes his heart against him, how does God's love abide in him?' The Eucharist determines the Christian manner of living the paschal mystery of Christ and the gift of Pentecost. Thanks to it, there occurs a profound transformation of human existence confronted always by temptation and suffering.

III. The Mystery of the Church

(1) The Body of Christ is unique. There exists, then, only one Church of God. The identity of one eucharistic assembly with another comes from the fact that all, with the same faith, celebrate the same memorial, that all by eating the same Body and sharing in the same Cup become the same unique Body of Christ into which they have been integrated by the same Baptism. If there are many celebrations, there is

nonetheless only one mystery celebrated in which all participate. Moreover, when the believer communicates in the Body and Blood of the Lord, he receives not a part of Christ but the whole Christ.

In the same way, the local church which celebrates the Eucharist gathered around the bishop is not a section of the Body of Christ. The multiplication of local *synaxes* does not divide the Church, but rather shows sacramentally its unity. Like the community of the apostles gathered around Christ, each eucharistic assembly is truly the holy Church of God, the Body of Christ, in communion with the first community of the disciples and with all those [communities] throughout the world which celebrate and have celebrated the Memorial of the Lord. It is also in communion with the assembly of the saints in heaven, which each celebration evokes.

(2) Far from excluding diversity or plurality, *koinonia* supposes it and heals the wounds of division, transcending the latter in unity.

Since Christ is one for the many, so, in the Church which is his Body, the one and the many, the universal and local, are necessarily simultaneous. Still more radically, because the one and only God is the communion of three Persons, the one and only Church is a communion of many communities and the local church a communion of persons. The one and only Church is identified with the *koinonia* of the churches. Unity and multiplicity appear so linked that one could not exist without the other. It is this relationship constitutive of the Church that institutions make visible and, so to speak, historicise.

(3) Since the catholic Church manifests itself in the *synaxis* of the local church, two conditions must be fulfilled above all if the local church which celebrates

the Eucharist is to be truly within the ecclesial communion.

a) The identity of the mystery of the Church lived by the local church with the mystery of the Church lived by the early Church – catholicity in time – is indeed fundamental. The Church is apostolic because it is founded and continually sustained in the mystery of salvation revealed in Jesus Christ and transmitted in the Spirit by those who were his witnesses, the apostles. Its members will be judged by Christ and the apostles (cf Lk 22:30).

b) Mutual recognition, today, between this local church and the other churches is also of capital importance. Each must recognise in the others, through local particularities, the identity of the mystery of the Church. It is a question of mutual recognition of catholicity as communion in the integrity of the mystery. This recognition is achieved first of all at the regional level. Communion in the same patriarchate, or in some other form of regional unity, is first of all a manifestation of the life of the Spirit in the same culture or in the same historical conditions. It equally implies unity of witness and calls for the exercise of fraternal correction in humility. This communion within the same region should extend itself further into communion between sister Churches.

This mutual recognition, however, is true only under the conditions expressed in the *Anaphora* of St John Chrysostom and the first Antiochene *anaphoras*. The first condition is communion in the same kerygma, so the same faith. Already contained in Baptism, this requirement is made explicit in the eucharistic celebration. But also required is the will for communion in love (*agape*) and in service (*diakonia*), not only in words but in deeds.

Permanence through history and mutual recognition alike are particularly evoked in the eucharistic *synaxis* by the mention, in the Canon, of the saints and, in the diptychs, of the heads of the churches. Thus it is understood why the latter are signs of catholic unity in eucharistic communion, responsible, each at his own level, for maintaining communion in the universal harmony of the churches and their common fidelity to the apostolic tradition.

(4) We find, then, among these churches the bonds of *communion* that the New Testament indicates: *communion* in faith, hope and love, *communion* in the sacraments, *communion* in the diversity of charisms, *communion* in reconciliation and *communion* in ministry. The agent of this *communion* is the Spirit of the risen Lord. Through him, the universal, catholic Church integrates diversity or plurality, by making of it one of its own essential elements. This catholicity represents the fulfilment of the prayer in Chapter 17 of the Gospel according to John, taken up in the eucharistic *epicleses*.

Attachment to apostolic communion binds all the bishops maintaining *episkope* [oversight] of local churches to the college of the apostles. They themselves form a college rooted by the Spirit in the 'once and for all' of the apostolic group, the unique witness of faith. This means not only that they must be united among themselves by faith, charity, mission and reconciliation, but also that they have in common the same responsibility and the same service of the Church. Because the one and only Church is realised in his local church, each bishop cannot separate care for his own church from care for the universal Church. And when, by the sacrament of ordination, he receives the charism of the Spirit for the *episkope* of a local church, his own, by that very fact he receives the charism of the Spirit for the *episkope* of the entire Church. In the people of God, he exercises it in *communion* with all the bishops who, here and now, are in charge of churches and in *communion* with the living tradition which the bishops of the past have handed on. The presence of bishops from neighbouring sees at his episcopal ordination 'sacramentalises' and actualises this *communion*. It produces a thorough fusion between his solicitude for the local community and care for the Church spread throughout the world. The *episkope* of the universal Church is entrusted by the Spirit to the totality of local bishops in *communion* with one another. This *communion* is expressed traditionally in conciliar practice. We shall have to examine further the way in which the latter is conceived and realised in the perspective of what we have just explained.

Faith, Sacraments
and the Unity of the Church
*(Bari, 1987)**

Introduction

(1) After our meeting in Munich in 1982 and in accordance with the *Plan* adopted by our Commission during its first meeting at Rhodes in 1980, this fourth session of the Commission has undertaken to consider the question of the relation between faith and sacramental communion.

(2) As was set down in the *Plan* of our dialogue, which was approved at Rhodes, unity of faith is a presupposition for unity in the sacraments and especially in the Holy Eucharist. But this commonly accepted principle raises some fundamental issues which require consideration. Does faith amount to adhering to formulas or is it also something else? Faith, which is a divine gift, should be understood as a commitment of the Christian, a commitment of his mind, his heart and his will. In its profound reality, it is also an ecclesial event, which is realised and accomplished in and through the communion of the Church, in its liturgical and especially in its eucharistic expression. This ecclesial and liturgical character of faith must be taken seriously into consideration.

(3) Given this fundamental character of faith, it is necessary to affirm that faith must be taken as a preliminary condition, already complete in itself, prior to

---

* This second agreed statement was finalised at the second session of the fourth plenary meeting of the international dialogue, held from 9 to 16 June, 1987, at the Oasis Santa-Maria, Cassano delle Murge, Bari, Italy.

sacramental communion; and also that it is increased by sacramental communion, which is the expression of the very life of the Church and the means of the spiritual growth of each of its members. This issue has to be raised in order to avoid a deficient approach to the problem of faith as a condition for unity. It should not, however, serve to obscure the fact that faith is such a condition, and that there cannot be sacramental communion without communion in faith, both in the broad sense and in the sense of dogmatic formulation.

(4) In addition to the question of faith as a presupposition of sacramental communion and in close connection with it, following the *Plan* of the dialogue, we have also considered in our meetings the relation of what are called the sacraments of initiation – i.e. Baptism, Confirmation or Chrismation and the Eucharist – to each other and to the unity of the Church. At this point, it is necessary to examine if our two Churches are confronted simply with a difference in liturgical practice or also in doctrine, given that liturgical practice and doctrine are linked to one another. Should we consider these three sacraments as belonging to one sacramental reality or as three autonomous sacramental acts? It should also be asked whether, for the sacraments of initiation, a difference in liturgical practice between the two traditions raises a problem of doctrinal divergence, which could be considered as a serious obstacle to unity.

I. Faith and Communion in the Sacraments

(5) Faith is inseparably both the gift of God who reveals Himself and the response of the man who receives this gift. It is the synergy of the grace of God

and human freedom. The locus of this communion is the Church. In the Church, revealed truth is transmitted according to the tradition of the apostles, based on Scripture, by the ecumenical councils, the liturgical life and the Fathers of the Church, and it is put into practice by the members of the Body of Christ. The faith of the Church constitutes the norm and the criterion for the personal act of faith. Faith is the result not of a logical elaboration and necessity, but of the influence of the grace of the Holy Spirit. The apostle Paul received grace 'in the obedience of faith' (Rom 1:5). Saint Basil says on this subject: 'Faith precedes discourses about God; faith and not demonstration. Being above logical methods, faith leads to consent. Faith is born not of geometric necessities, but of the energies of the Spirit' (*In Ps.* 115,1).

(6) Every sacrament presupposes and expresses the faith of the Church which celebrates it. Indeed, in a sacrament, the Church does more than profess and express its faith: it makes present the mystery it is celebrating. The Holy Spirit reveals the Church as the Body of Christ which he constitutes and makes grow. Thus, through the sacraments, the Church nourishes and develops the communion of faith of its members.

1. True faith is a divine gift and man's free response

(7) Faith is a gift of the Holy Spirit. Through faith, God grants salvation. Through it, humanity has access to the mystery of Christ who constitutes the Church and whom the Church communicates through the Holy Spirit who dwells in it. The Church cannot but transmit what causes it to exist. Now, there is only one mystery of Christ and God's gift is unique, whole and irrevoca-

ble (Rom 11:29). As for its content, faith embraces the totality of the doctrine and practice of the Church relating to salvation. Dogma, conduct and liturgical life overlap each other to form a single whole and together constitute the treasure of faith. Linking in a remarkable fashion the theoretical and practical character of faith, Saint John Damascene says: 'This [faith] is made perfect by all that Christ decreed, faith through works, respect for and practice of the commandments of the One who has renewed us. Indeed, he who does not believe according to the tradition of the catholic Church, or who by unseemly works is in communion with the devil, is an infidel.' (*De fide orthodoxa* IV, 10, 83)

(8) Given by God, the faith announced by the Church is proclaimed, lived and transmitted in a local, visible church in communion with all the local churches spread over the world, that is, the catholic Church of all times and everywhere. Man is integrated into the Body of Christ by his *koinonia* [communion] with this visible Church which, by means of the sacramental life and the Word of God, nourishes in him this faith and in which the Holy Spirit works in him.

(9) One can say that, in this way, the gift of faith exists in the one Church in its concrete historical situation, determined by the environment and the times, and therefore in each and all of believers under the guidance of their pastors. By means of human language and in a variety of cultural and historical expressions, man must remain always faithful to this gift of faith. Certainly, one cannot claim that the expression of true faith, transmitted and lived in the celebration of the sacraments, exhausts the totality of the richness of the mystery revealed in Jesus Christ. Nevertheless, within the limits of its formulation and of the persons who receive it, it gives access to the whole

truth of revealed faith, that is, to the fulness of salvation and life in the Holy Spirit.

(10) According to the Letter to the Hebrews, this faith is 'the substance of things hoped for, the vision of unseen realities' (11:1). It grants a share in divine goods. It is understood also in terms of an existential confidence in the power and love of God, in acceptance of the eschatological promises as fulfilled in the person of the Lord Jesus Christ. Yet, as this Letter to the Hebrews further indicates, faith also requires an attitude regarding existence and the world. This attitude is marked by readiness to sacrifice one's own will and to offer one's life to God and to others as Christ did on the cross. Faith brings one into association with the witness of Christ and with 'the cloud of witnesses' (12:1) who surround the Church.

(11) Faith therefore involves a conscious and free response on the part of man and a continual change of heart and spirit. Consequently, faith is an interior change and a transformation, causing one to live in the grace of the Holy Spirit who renews man. It seeks a reorientation towards the realities of the Kingdom which is coming and which, even now, is beginning to transform the realities of this world.

(12) Faith is a presupposition of Baptism and of the entire sacramental life which follows it. Through Baptism, one actually participates in the death and resurrection of Jesus Christ (Rom 6). Thus begins a process which continues through the whole of Christian existence.

2. *The liturgical expression of faith*

(13) In the Church, the sacraments are the place where faith is lived, transmitted and professed *par*

excellence. In the Byzantine liturgical tradition, the first prayer for entrance into the catechumenate asks the Lord for the candidate: 'Fill him with faith, hope and love for you, so that he may understand that you are the one true God, with your only Son, our Lord Jesus Christ and your Holy Spirit.' Likewise, the first question that the Church puts to a candidate for Baptism in the Latin liturgical tradition is: 'What do you ask of the Church?' and the candidate answers: 'Faith.' – 'What does faith give you?' – 'Eternal life.'

(14) Our two Churches express their conviction in this matter by the axiom: '*Lex orandi lex credendi*'. For them, the liturgical tradition is the authentic interpreter of revelation and hence the criterion for the profession of true faith. Indeed, it is in the liturgical expression of the faith of our Churches that the witness of the Fathers and of the ecumenical councils celebrated together continues to be for believers the sure guide of faith. Independently of diversity in theological expression, this witness, which itself renders explicit the 'kerygma' of the holy Scriptures, is made present in liturgical celebration. For its part, the faith proclaimed nourishes the liturgical prayer of the people of God.

3. The Holy Spirit and the sacraments

(15) The sacraments of the Church are 'sacraments of faith' where God the Father hears the *epiclesis* [invocation] in which the Church expresses its faith by this prayer for the coming of the Spirit. In them, the Father gives his Holy Spirit who leads [us] into the fulness of salvation in Christ. Christ himself constitutes the Church as his Body. The Holy Spirit edifies the Church. There is no gift in the Church which

cannot be attributed to the Spirit (Basil the Great, *PG* 30, 289). The sacraments are the gift and grace of the Holy Spirit, in Jesus Christ in the Church. This is expressed very concisely in an Orthodox hymn for Pentecost: 'The Holy Spirit is the author of every gift. He makes prophecies spring forth. He renders priests perfect. He teaches wisdom to the ignorant. From fishermen he makes theologians and he consolidates the institution of the Church.'

(16) Every sacrament of the Church confers the grace of the Holy Spirit by being inseparably a sign recalling what God has accomplished in the past, a sign manifesting what he is effecting in the believer and in the Church and a sign announcing and anticipating eschatological fulfilment. In sacramental celebration, the Church thus manifests, illustrates, and confesses its faith in the unity of God's design.

(17) It will be noted that all the sacraments have an essential relationship with the Eucharist. The Eucharist is the proclamation of faith *par excellence*, from which is derived and to which is ordered every confession. Indeed, it alone proclaims fully, in the presence of the Lord which the power of the Spirit brings about, the marvel of the divine work. For the Lord sacramentally makes his work pass into the Church's celebration. The sacraments of the Church transmit grace, express and strengthen faith in Jesus Christ and are thus witnesses of faith.

4. Faith formulated and celebrated in the sacraments: symbols of faith

(18) In the eucharistic assembly, the Church celebrates the event of the mystery of salvation in the

eucharistic prayer (*anaphora*) for the glory of God. The mystery it celebrates is the very one which it confesses, while receiving the saving gift.

(19) Although the content and finality of this eucharistic celebration have remained the same in the local churches, the latter have nevertheless used varied formulas and different languages which, according to the genius of different cultures, bring into relief particular aspects and implications of the unique salvation-event. At the heart of ecclesial life, in the eucharistic *synaxis* [assembly], our two traditions – eastern and western – thus experience a certain diversity in the formulation of the content of the faith being celebrated.

(20) From earliest times, there has been joined to the administration of Baptism a formulation of faith by means of which the local church transmits to the catechumen the essential content of the doctrine of the apostles. This symbol of faith enunciates in compact form the essentials of the apostolic tradition, articulated chiefly in the confession of faith in the Holy Trinity and in the Church. When all the local churches confess the true faith, they transmit, in the rite of Baptism, this one faith in the Father, Son and Holy Spirit. Nevertheless, at different times and in different places, the formulation has been expressed differently as circumstances required, using terms and propositions which were not identical from one formulary to another. All, however, respected the content of faith.

The eastern Church in its baptismal rite uses the Nicene-Constantinopolitan creed. Faithful to its own tradition, the western Church transmits to the catechumen the so-called 'Apostles' Creed'. This diversity of formulas from one Church to another does not in itself indicate any divergence regarding the content of the faith transmitted and lived.

5. Conditions for communion of faith

(21) The first condition for a true communion between the Churches is that each Church makes reference to the Nicene-Constantinopolitan creed as the necessary norm of this communion of the one Church spread throughout the world and across the ages. In this sense, true faith is presupposed for communion in the sacraments. Communion is possible only between Churches which have faith, priesthood and the sacraments in common. It is because of this reciprocal recognition that the faith handed down in each local church is one and the same (as are the priesthood and the sacrament besides), that they recognise each other as genuine churches of God and that each of the faithful is welcomed by the churches as a brother or sister in faith. At the same time, however, faith is deepened and clarified by the ecclesial communion lived in the sacraments in each community. This ecclesial qualification of faith as the fruit of sacramental life is verified at various levels of Church life.

(22) In the first place, by the celebration of the sacraments, the assembly proclaims, transmits and assimilates its faith.

(23) Furthermore, in the celebration of the sacraments, each local church expresses its profound nature. It is in continuity with the Church of the apostles and in communion with all the churches which share one and the same faith and celebrate the same sacraments. In the sacramental celebration of a local church, the other local churches recognise the identity of their faith with that church's and by that fact are strengthened in their own life of faith. Thus the celebration of the sacraments confirms the communion of faith between the churches and manifests it. This is why a

member of one local church, baptised in that church, can receive the sacraments in another local church. This communion in the sacraments expresses the identity and unicity of the true faith which the churches share.

(24) In eucharistic concelebration by representatives of different local churches, identity of faith is particularly manifested and reinforced by the sacramental act itself. That is why councils, in which bishops led by the Holy Spirit express the truth of the Church's faith, are always associated with the eucharistic celebration. By proclaiming the one mystery of Christ and sharing in the one sacramental communion, bishops, clergy and the whole Christian people united with them are able to witness to the faith of the Church.

6. *True faith and communion in the sacraments*

(25) Identity of faith, then, is an essential element of ecclesial communion in the celebration of the sacraments. However, a certain diversity in its formulation does not compromise the *koinonia* between local churches when each church can recognise, under the variety of formulations, the one authentic faith received from the apostles.

(26) During the centuries of the undivided Church, diversity in the theological expression of a doctrine did not endanger sacramental communion. After the schism occurred, East and West continued to develop, but they did so separately from one other. Thus it was no longer possible for them to take unanimous decisions that were valid for both of them.

(27) The Church as 'pillar and bulwark of truth' (1Tim 3:25) keeps the deposit of faith pure and unal-

tered while transmitting it faithfully to its members. When the authentic teaching or unity of the Church were threatened by heresy or schism, the Church, basing itself on the Bible, the living tradition and the decisions of preceding councils, declared the correct faith authentically and infallibly in an ecumenical council.

(28) When it is established that differences represent a rejection of earlier dogmas of the Church and are not simple differences of theological expression, then clearly one is faced with a true division about faith. It is no longer possible to have sacramental communion. For faith must be confessed in words which express the truth itself. However, the life of the Church may occasion new verbal expressions of the faith 'once and for all delivered to the saints' (Jude 3), if new historical and cultural needs call for them, as long as there is explicit desire not to change the content of the doctrine itself. In such cases, the verbal expression can become normative for unanimity in faith. This requires criteria for judgement enabling a distinction between legitimate developments, under the inspiration of the Holy Spirit, and other ones.

Thus:

(29) The continuity of tradition: the Church ought to give suitable answers to new problems, answers based on Scripture and in accord and essential continuity with previous statements of dogmas.

(30) The doxological meaning of faith: every liturgical development in one local church should be able to be seen by the others as in conformity with the mystery of salvation such as that church has received it and celebrates it.

(31) The soteriological meaning of faith: every expression of faith should envisage the final destiny of

man, as a child of God by grace, in his deification [*theosis*] through victory over death and in the transfiguration of creation.

(32) If a formulation of faith contradicts one or other of these criteria, it becomes an obstacle to communion. If, on the other hand, some particular formulation of faith contradicts none of these criteria, then this formulation can be considered as a legitimate expression of faith, not one making sacramental communion impossible.

(33) This requires that the theology of *theologoumena* [legitimate interpretations of articles of faith] be seriously considered. It is also necessary to clarify what concrete development occurring in one part of Christianity can be considered by the other as a legitimate development. Furthermore, it should be recognised that often the meaning of terms has changed in the course of time. For this reason, an effort should be made to understand every formula according to the intention of its authors so as not to introduce into it foreign elements, nor to exclude elements which, in the mind of the authors, were obvious.

7. The unity of the Church in faith and the sacraments

(34) In the Church, the function of ministers is above all to maintain, guarantee and promote the growth of communion in faith and the sacraments. As ministers of the sacraments and doctors of the faith, the bishops, assisted by other ministers, proclaim the faith of the Church, explain its content and its demands for Christian life and defend it against wrong interpretations which would falsify or compromise the truth of the mystery of salvation.

(35) Charitable works of ministers, or their taking positions on the problems of a given time or place, are inseparable from the two functions of the proclamation and teaching of the faith, on the one hand, and the celebration of worship and the sacraments, on the other.

(36) Thus, unity of faith within a local church and between local churches is guaranteed and judged by the bishop, who is the witness to tradition, in communion with his people. It is inseparable from unity in sacramental life. Communion in faith and communion in the sacraments are not two distinct realities. They are two aspects of a single reality which the Holy Spirit fosters, increases and safeguards among the faithful.

II. The Sacraments of Christian Initiation: their Relation to the Unity of the Church

(37) Christian initiation is a unity in which Chrismation is the perfection of Baptism and the Eucharist is the completion of both.

The unity of Baptism, Chrismation and the Eucharist in a single sacramental reality does not deny, however, their specific character. Thus, Baptism in water and the Spirit is participation in the death and resurrection of Christ and new birth by grace. Chrismation is the gift of the Spirit to the baptised as a personal gift. Received under the proper conditions, the Eucharist, through communion in the Body and Blood of the Lord, grants participation in the Kingdom of God, including the forgiveness of sins, communion in the divine life itself and membership of the eschatological community.

(38) The history of the baptismal rites in East and

West, as well as the way in which our common Fathers interpreted the doctrinal significance of the rites, show clearly that the sacraments of initiation form a unity. That unity is strongly affirmed by the Orthodox Church. For its part, the Catholic Church also maintains it. Thus, the new Roman Ritual of initiation declares that 'the three sacraments of Christian initiation closely combine to bring us, the faithful of Christ, to his full stature and to enable us to carry out the mission of the entire people of God in the Church and in the world' [Christian Initiation, General Introduction, no. 2; in *Rite of Christian Initiation of Adults* (Geoffrey Chapman, London, 1987)].

(39) The pattern of administration of the sacraments which developed very early in the Church reveals how the Church understood the various stages of initiation as accomplishing, theologically and liturgically, incorporation into Christ by entry into the Church and growth in him through communion in his Body and Blood in this Church. All of this is effected by the same Holy Spirit who constitutes the believer as a member of the Body of the Lord.

(40) The early pattern included the following elements.

(41) 1. For adults, a period of spiritual probation and instruction during which the catechumens were formed for their definitive incorporation into the Church.

(42) 2. Baptism by the bishop surrounded by the priests and deacons, or administered by priests assisted by deacons, preceded by a profession of faith and various intercessions and liturgical actions.

(43) 3. Confirmation or Chrismation by the bishop in the West, or by the priest, when the bishop was absent, in the East, by means of the imposition of hands and anointing with holy chrism, or by one of the two.

(44) 4. The celebration of the holy Eucharist during which the newly baptised and confirmed were admitted to full participation in the Body of Christ.

(45) These three sacraments were administered in the course of a single, complex liturgical celebration. There followed a period of further catechetical and spiritual maturation through instruction and frequent participation in the Eucharist.

(46) This pattern remains the ideal for both Churches, since it corresponds as exactly as possible to the appropriation of the scriptural and apostolic tradition accomplished by the early Christian churches which lived in full communion with each other.

(47) The Baptism of infants, which has been practised from the beginning, became in the Church the most usual procedure for introducing new Christians into the full life of the Church. On the other hand, certain local changes took place in liturgical practice in consideration of the pastoral needs of the faithful. These changes did not affect the theological understanding of the fundamental unity, in the Holy Spirit, of the whole process of Christian initiation.

(48) In the East, the temporal unity of the liturgical celebration of the three sacraments was retained, thus emphasising the unity of the work of the Holy Spirit and the fulness of the incorporation of the child into the sacramental life of the Church.

In the West, it was often preferred to delay Confirmation so as to retain contact between the baptised person and the bishop. Thus, priests were not ordinarily authorised to confirm.

(49) The essential points of doctrine on Baptism on which the two Churches are agreed are the following.

1. The necessity of Baptism for salvation.

2. The effects of Baptism, particularly new life in Christ and liberation from original sin.

3. Incorporation into the Church by Baptism.

4. The relation of Baptism to the mystery of the Trinity.

5. The essential link between Baptism and the death and resurrection of the Lord.

6. The role of the Holy Spirit in Baptism.

7. The necessity of water which manifests Baptism's character as the bath of new birth.

(50) On the other hand, differences concerning Baptism exist between the two Churches.

1. The fact that the Catholic Church, while recognising the primordial importance of Baptism by immersion, ordinarily practises Baptism by infusion.

2. The fact that in the Catholic Church a deacon can be the ordinary minister of Baptism.

(51) Moreover, in certain Latin churches, for pastoral reasons, for example in order better to prepare confirmands on the threshold of adolescence, little by little the practice has spread of admitting to first communion baptised persons who have not yet received Confirmation, even though the disciplinary directives which called for the traditional order of the sacraments of Christian initiation have never been abrogated. This inversion, which provokes objections or understandable reservations among both Orthodox and Roman Catholics, calls for deep theological and pastoral reflection because pastoral practice should never lose sight of the meaning of the early tradition and its doctrinal importance. It must be recalled here that Baptism conferred after the age of reason in the Latin Church is now always followed by Confirmation and participation in the Eucharist.

(52) At the same time, both Churches are pre-

occupied with the necessity of assuring the spiritual formation of the neophyte in the faith. For that, they wish to emphasise, on the one hand, that there is a necessary connection between the sovereign action of the Spirit, who realises through the three sacraments the full incorporation of the person into the life of the Church, the latter's response and that of his community of faith and, on the other hand, that the full illumination of faith is possible only when the neophyte, of whatever age, has received the sacraments of Christian initiation.

(53) Finally, it is recalled that the Council of Constantinople, jointly celebrated by the two Churches in 879-880, determined that each see would retain the ancient usages of its tradition, the Church of Rome preserving its own usages, the Church of Constantinople its own, and the thrones of the East also doing the same (cf Mansi XVII, 489 b).

The Sacrament of Order in the Sacramental Structure of the Church with particular reference to the importance of Apostolic Succession for the Sanctification and Unity of the People of God
*(Valamo, 1988)**

Introduction

(1) Having expressed our idea of the mystery of the Church as a communion of faith and sacraments, eminently manifested in the eucharistic celebration, our Commission now addresses the crucial question of the place and role of ordained ministry in the sacramental structure of the Church. We will deal, then, with the sacrament of Order as well as with ordination to each of the three degrees of episcopate, presbyterate and diaconate. We rely on the certitude that in our Churches apostolic succession is fundamental for the sanctification and unity of the people of God.

(2) Our Churches affirm that ministry in the Church makes present that of Christ himself. In the New Testament writings, Christ is called apostle, prophet, pastor, servant, *diakonos*, doctor, priest, *episkopos*. Our common tradition recognises the close link which exists between the work of Christ and that of the Holy Spirit.

(3) This understanding prevents us from seeing in the economy Christ in isolation from the Spirit. The actual presence of Christ in his Church is also of an

---

* This third agreed statement was finalised at the fifth plenary meeting of the international dialogue, held from 19 to 27 June, 1988, at Valamo Monastery in Finland.

eschatological nature, since the Spirit constitutes the earnest of the perfect realisation of God's design for the world.

(4) In this perspective, the Church appears as the community of the New Covenant which Christ through the Holy Spirit gathers around himself and builds up as his Body. Through the Church, Christ is present in history; through it he achieves the salvation of the world.

(5) Since Christ is present in the Church, it is his ministry that is carried out in it. Ministry in the Church, therefore, does not substitute for the ministry of Christ. It has its source in him. Since the Spirit sent by Christ gives life to the Church, ministry is fruitful only by the grace of the Holy Spirit. In fact, it includes many functions which the members of the community carry out according to the diversity of the gifts they receive as members of the Body of Christ. Certain members receive through ordination and exercise the function proper to the episcopate, the presbyterate and the diaconate. There is no Church without the ministries created by the Spirit; there are no ministries without the Church, that is to say outside and above the community. Ministries find their meaning and *raison d'être* only in it.

I. Christ and the Holy Spirit

(6) The Spirit, who eternally proceeds from the Father and reposes on the Son, prepared the Christ-event and achieved it. The incarnation of the Son of God, his death and his resurrection, were in fact accomplished according to the will of the Father, in the Holy Spirit. At [his] Baptism, the Father through the

manifestation of the Spirit inaugurates the mission of the Son. This Spirit is present in his ministry: to announce the Good News of salvation, to manifest the coming of the Kingdom and to bear witness to the Father. It is likewise in the same Spirit that, as the unique priest of the New Covenant, Christ offers the sacrifice of his own life and it is through the Spirit that he is glorified.

(7) Since Pentecost, in the Church which is his Body, it is only in the Spirit that those who are charged with ministry can carry out the acts which bring the Body to its full stature. In the ministry of Christ as in that of the Church, it is one and the same Spirit who is at work and who will act with us all the days of our life.

(8) In the Church, ministry should be lived in holiness, with a view towards the sanctification of the people of God. So that the whole Church and especially its ordained ministers might be able to contribute to 'the perfecting of the saints in the work of ministry, for building up the Body of Christ', different services are made possible by many charisms (Eph 4:11-12; cf 1 Cor 12:4-28; Rom 12:4-8).

(9) The newness of the Church's ministry consists in this: Christ, servant of God for humanity, is present through the Spirit, in the Church, his Body, from which he cannot be separated. For he himself is 'the first-born of many brothers'. It is in this sacramental way that one must understand the work of Christ in history from Pentecost to the Parousia. The ministry of the Church as such is sacramental.

(10) For this reason, Christ's presence in the Church is also eschatological. Wherever the Spirit is at work, he actually reveals to the world the presence of the Kingdom in creation. Here is where ecclesial ministry is rooted.

(11) This ecclesial ministry is by nature sacramental. The term sacramental is meant to emphasise here that every ministry is bound to the eschatological reality of the Kingdom. The grace of the Holy Spirit, as earnest of the world to come, has its source in the death and resurrection of Christ and is offered, in a sacramental manner, by means of sensible realities. The term sacramental likewise shows that the minister is a member of the community whom the Spirit invests with specific functions and power to assemble the latter and to preside in the name of Christ over the acts in which it celebrates the mysteries of salvation. This view of the sacramentality of ministry is rooted in the fact that Christ is made present in the Church by the Spirit whom he himself has sent to the Church.

(12) This nature of ecclesial ministry is further shown by the fact that all ministries are intended to serve the world so as to lead it to its true goal, the Kingdom of God. It is by constituting the eschatological community as [the] Body of Christ that the ministry of the Church answers the needs of the world.

(13) The community gathered in the Spirit around Christ exercising his ministry has its foundation in Christ, who is himself the cornerstone, and in the community of the Twelve. The apostolic character of churches and their ministry is understood in this light.

(14) On one hand, the Twelve are the witnesses of the historic life of Jesus, of his ministry and of his resurrection. On the other, as associates of the glorified Christ, they link each community with the community of the last days. Ecclesial ministry will thus be called apostolic because it is carried out in continuity with and in fidelity to what was given by Christ and handed on in history by the apostles. But it will also be apostolic because the eucharistic assembly at which

the minister presides is an anticipation of the final community with Christ. Through this double relationship, the Church's ministry remains constantly bound to that of the Twelve, and thereby to that of Christ.

II. The Priesthood in the Economy of Salvation

(15) The entire divine economy culminates in the incarnation of the Son, in his teaching, his passion, his glorious resurrection, his ascension and his second coming. Christ acts in the Holy Spirit. Thus, once and for all, there is laid the foundation for re-establishing the communion of man with God.

(16) According to the Letter to the Hebrews, Christ by his death has become the one mediator of the New Covenant (Heb 9:15) and, having entered once and for all into the Holy Place with his own Blood (Heb 9:12), he is forever in heaven the one and eternal High Priest of this New Covenant, 'so as to appear now in the presence of God on our behalf' (Heb 9:24) to offer his sacrifice (Heb 10:12).

(17) Invisibly present in the Church through the Holy Spirit, whom he has sent, Christ is then its unique High Priest. In him, the priest and victim, all together, pastors and faithful, form 'a chosen race, a royal priesthood, a holy nation, a people set apart' (1 Pet 2:9; cf Rev 5:10).

(18) All members of the Church, as members of the Body of Christ, participate in his priesthood and are called to become 'a living sacrifice, holy and acceptable to God' (Rom 12:1; cf 1Pet 2:5). To make himself present, Christ, the Head of the Church, established apostles chosen from among the people, whom he endowed with authority and power by strengthening

them through the grace of the Holy Spirit. The work and mission of the apostles are continued in the Church by the bishops with the priests and deacons who assist them. Bishops are established by ordination as successors of the apostles and they direct the people along the ways of salvation.

(19) Around the glorified Lord, the Twelve give witness to the presence of the Kingdom already inaugurated, which will be fully manifested at the second coming. Christ, indeed, promised them that they would sit on twelve thrones, to judge with the Son of Man the twelve tribes of Israel (Mt 19:28).

(20) As historical witnesses of what the Lord accomplished, the ministry of the Twelve is unique and irreplaceable. What they laid down was founded therefore once and for all, and no one in the future will be able to build except on the foundation thus established (Eph 2:20; Rev 21:14).

(21) But, at the same time, the apostles remain the foundations of the Church as it endures through the ages, in such a way that the mission they received from the Lord remains always visible and active, in expectation of the Lord's return (cf Mt 18:18 and, earlier, 16:19).

(22) That is why the Church, in which the grace of God is at work, is itself the sacrament *par excellence*, the manifestation, in advance, of the final realities and the foretaste of God's Kingdom, of the glory of Him who is God and Father and of the *eschaton* in history.

(23) Within this sacrament which is the Church, the priesthood conferred by ordination and given for this Church finds its place. In fact, it constitutes in the Church a charismatic ministry (*leitourgêma*) *par excellence*. It is at the service of the Church's life and

continued existence by the Holy Spirit, that is to say, of the unity in Christ of all the faithful living and dead, of the martyrs, the saints and the just of the Old Testament.

III. The Ministry of the Bishop, of the Presbyter and of the Deacon

(24) In the celebration of the Eucharist, the entire assembly, each one in his place, is *leitourgos* of the *koinonia*, and is such only by the Spirit [cf *Munich Document*, II,2; above, p. 45]. 'There is a variety of ministries, but the same Lord.... To each is given the manifestation of the Spirit for the common good' (1 Cor 12:5,7). The various ministries converge in the eucharistic synaxis, in the course of which they are conferred. However, their diversity is ordered to the entire life of the community: fidelity to the Word of God, abiding in harmony and fraternal charity, witness before 'those outside', growth in holiness, constancy in prayer and care for the poorest.

(25) With its culmination in the celebration of the Eucharist, in which is completed the Christian initiation by which all become [the] one Body of Christ, the ministry of the bishop is, among all the charisms and ministries which the Spirit raises up, a ministry of presiding for gathering in unity. In fact, bearing the variety of gifts of the Spirit, the local church has at its centre the bishop, whose communion realises the unity of all and expresses the fulness of the Church.

(26) This unity of the local church is inseparable from the universal communion of the churches. It is essential for a church to be in communion with the others. This communion is expressed and realised in and through the episcopal college. By his ordination,

the bishop is constituted as minister of a church which he represents in the universal communion.

(27) Episcopal ordination, which, according to the canons, is conferred by at least two or three bishops, expresses the communion of the churches with that of the person selected: it makes him a member of the communion of bishops. In ordination, the bishops exercise their function as witnesses to communion in apostolic faith and sacramental life, not only with regard to him whom they ordain, but also with regard to the church of which he will be bishop. What is fundamental for the incorporation of the newly elected person into episcopal communion is that it is accomplished by the glorified Lord in the power of the Holy Spirit at the moment of the imposition of hands.

Here we are considering ordination only under its sacramental aspect. The problems raised by the manner of election will be studied later.

(28) Episcopal ordination confers on the one who receives it by the gift of the Spirit the fulness of the priesthood. At the time of ordination, the concelebration of the bishops expresses the unity of the Church and its identity with the apostolic community. They impose hands and invoke the Holy Spirit on the one who will be ordained, as the only ones qualified to confer upon him the episcopal ministry. They do so, however, within the setting of the prayer of the community.

(29) By his ordination, the bishop receives all the powers necessary for fulfilling his function. The canonical conditions for the exercise of his function and the installation of the bishop in the local church will be further discussed by the Commission.

(30) The gift conferred consecrates the recipient to the service of the Church in a definitive way. This is a point of the traditional doctrine in East and West,

which is confirmed by the fact that, in the event of disciplinary sanctions against a bishop followed by canonical reintegration, there is no re-ordination. On this subject, as on all the essential points concerning ordination, our Churches have a common doctrine and practice, even if on certain canonical and disciplinary requirements, such as celibacy, customs can be different for pastoral and spiritual reasons.

(31) But ecclesial ministry is exercised through a variety of functions. These are carried out in interdependence; none could replace another. This is especially true of the fundamental ministries of the bishop, the presbyter and the deacon, and of the functions of the laity, all of which together give structure to the eucharistic community.

(32) Throughout the entire history of our Churches, women have played a fundamental role, as witness not only the most Holy Mother of God, the holy women mentioned in the New Testament and the numerous women saints whom we venerate, but also so many other women who to the present day have served the Church in many ways. Their particular charisms are very important for the building up of the Body of Christ. But our Churches remain faithful to the historical and theological tradition according to which they ordain only men to the priestly ministry.

(33) Just as the apostles gathered together the first communities by proclaiming Christ, celebrating the Eucharist and leading the baptised towards growing communion with Christ and with each other, so the bishop, established by the same Spirit, continues to preach the same Gospel, to preside at the same Eucharist and to serve the unity and sanctification of the same community. He is thus the icon of Christ the servant among his brethren.

(34) Because it is at the Eucharist that the Church manifests its fulness, it is equally in presiding at the Eucharist that the role of the bishop and of the priest appears in its full light.

(35) In the eucharistic celebration, believers actually offer themselves with Christ as a royal priesthood. They do so thanks to the ministerial action which makes present in their midst Christ himself who proclaims the Word, makes the bread and the cup become through the Spirit his Body and Blood, incorporating them into himself and giving them his life. Moreover, the prayer and the offering of the people incorporated in Christ are, as it were, recapitulated in the thanksgiving prayer of the bishop and his offering of the gifts.

(36) The Eucharist thus realises the unity of the Christian community. It also manifests the unity of all the churches which celebrate it in truth and, further still, the unity across the centuries of all the churches with the apostolic community from the beginning up to the present day. In the Spirit, it brings together across history the great assembly of the apostles, the martyrs and the witnesses of all periods gathered around the Lamb. This, the central act of the episcopal ministry, thus makes already present the world to come: the Church gathered in communion, offering itself to the Father, through the Son, in the Holy Spirit.

(37) He who presides at the Eucharist is responsible for preserving communion in fidelity to the teaching of the apostles and for guiding it in the new life. He is its servant and pastor. The bishop is also the guide of the entire liturgical life of his local church and, following his example, it becomes a community of prayer. He presides at its praise and at its intercession, and he himself prays unceasingly for all those entrusted to

him by the Lord, knowing that he is responsible for each one before the tribunal of God.

(38) It also rests with him to see to it that there is given to his people, by preaching and catechesis, the authentic content of the Word of God given to the apostles 'once and for all'. He is, in fact, the primary one responsible for the preaching of the Word of God in his diocese.

(39) Also to him belongs the task of leading this people towards proclaiming salvation in Jesus Christ to all men and towards a witness which embodies that proclamation. Therefore, it falls to him to govern his church in such a way that it remains always faithful to its Christian vocation and to the mission deriving therefrom. In all this, however, he remains a member of the Church called to holiness and dependent on the salvific ministry of this Church, as St Augustine reminds his community: 'For you I am a bishop, with you I am a Christian.' At his ordination, the bishop makes his own the faith of the whole Church by solemnly confessing it and thus becomes a father to the extent that he has fully become its son by this confession. It is essential for the bishop to be the father of his people.

(40) As successors of the apostles, bishops are responsible for communion in apostolic faith and for fidelity to the demands of a life lived according to the Gospel.

(41) It is in presiding over the eucharistic assembly that the role of the bishop finds its accomplishment. Presbyters form the college which surrounds him during this celebration. They exercise the responsibilities that the bishop entrusts to them by celebrating the sacraments, teaching the Word of God and governing the community in profound and continuous commun-

ion with him. The deacon, for his part, is engaged in the service of the bishop and the priest and acts as a link between them and the assembly of the faithful.

(42) The priest, ordained by the bishop and dependent upon him, is sent to perform certain definite tasks; above all, he is sent to a parish community to be its pastor: he presides over the Eucharist at the altar (consecrated by the bishop), he is minister of the sacraments for the community, he preaches the Gospel and catechises and it is his duty to keep in unity the charisms of the people (*laos*) of God; he appears as the ordinary minister of the local eucharistic community, and the diocese is thus a communion of eucharistic communities.

(43) The diaconate is exercised at the service of the bishop and the presbyter, in the liturgy, in the work of evangelisation and in the service of charity.

IV. Apostolic Succession

(44) The one and only ministry of Christ and his apostles remains active in history. This action is, through the Spirit, a breakthrough of 'the world to come', in fidelity to what the apostles transmitted of what Jesus did and taught.

(45) The importance of this succession comes also from the fact that apostolic tradition concerns the community and not only an isolated individual, ordained bishop. Apostolic succession is transmitted through local churches ('in each city', according to the expression of Eusebius; 'by reason of their consanguinity of doctrine', according to Tertullian in the *De Praescriptione*, 32,6). It is a question of a succession of persons in the community, because the *Una Sancta*

is a communion of local churches and not of isolated individuals. It is within this mystery of *koinonia* that the episcopate appears as the focal point of apostolic succession.

(46) According to what we have already said in the Munich Document: 'Apostolic succession, therefore, means something more than a mere transmission of powers. It is succession in a church which witnesses to the apostolic faith, in *communion* with the other churches which witness to the same apostolic faith. The see (*cathedra*) plays an essential role in inserting the bishop into the heart of ecclesial apostolicity' (*Munich Document*, II,4; above, p. 47). We [would] explain that the term '*cathedra*' is used here in the sense of the presence of the bishop in each local church.

(47) 'On the other hand, once ordained, the bishop becomes in his church the guarantor of apostolicity, the one who represents it within the *communion* of churches and its link with other churches. That is why, in his church, any Eucharist can be celebrated *in truth* only if presided over by him or by a presbyter *in communion* with him. Mention of him in the *anaphora* is essential.' (*id*; above, pp. 47-48.)

(48) 'Attachment to apostolic communion binds all the bishops maintaining *episkope* of local churches to the college of the apostles' (*ibid.*, III,4; above, p. 51). The bishops are thus rooted in the 'once and for all' of the apostolic group through which the Holy Spirit gives witness to faith. Indeed, as the foundation of the Church, the Twelve are unique. Even so, it was necessary that other men should make visible their irreplaceable presence. In this way, the link of each community would be maintained both with the original community and with the eschatological community.

(49) By his ordination, each bishop becomes a successor of the apostles, whatever may be the church over which he presides or the prerogatives (*presbeia*) of this church among the other churches.

(50) Incorporated into the number of those to whom particular responsibility for the ministry of salvation has been entrusted, and so placed in the succession of the apostles, the bishop must pass on their teaching as well as modelling his whole life on them. Irenaeus of Lyons puts it thus: 'It is where the charisms of God have been planted that we should be instructed in the truth, that is, from those in whom are united succession in the Church from the apostles, unassailable integrity of conduct and incorruptible purity of doctrine' (*Adv. Haer.*, IV,26,5). Among the essential functions of the bishop is that of being, in his church, through the Spirit, a witness and guarantor of faith and an instrument for maintaining it in apostolic fidelity. Apostolic succession is also a succession in the labours and sufferings of the apostles in service of the Gospel and in defence of the people entrusted to each bishop. According to the words of the First Letter of St Peter, apostolic succession is also a succession in the presence of mercy and of understanding, of defence of the weak and of constant attention to those entrusted to their charge, the bishop thereby becoming a model for the flock (cf 1Pet 5:1-4; 2Cor 4:8-11; 1Tim 4:12; Tit 2:7).

(51) Furthermore, it belongs to the episcopal ministry to articulate and organise the life of the Church with its services and offices. It falls to him also to watch over the choice of those who are to carry out responsibilities in his diocese. Fraternal communion requires that all the members, ministers or lay people, listen to each other for the good of the people of God.

(52) In the course of its history, the Church in East and West has known various forms of practising communion among bishops: by exchanges of letters, by visits from one church to another, but principally by synodal or conciliar life. From the first centuries, a distinction and a hierarchy were established between churches of earlier foundation and churches of more recent foundation, between mother churches and daughter churches and between churches of larger cities and churches of outlying areas. This hierarchy or *taxis* soon found its canonical expression, formulated by the councils, especially in the canons which were received by all the churches of East and West. These are, in the first place, canons 6 and 7 of the First Council of Nicea (325), canon 3 of the First Council of Constantinople (the second ecumenical council, 381), canon 28 of Chalcedon (the fourth ecumenical council, 451), as well as canons 3, 4 and 5 of Sardica (343) and the first canon of the Council of Santa Sophia (879-880). Even if these canons have not always been interpreted in the same way in East and West, they belong to the heritage of the Church. They assigned to bishops occupying certain metropolitan or major sees a place and recognised prerogatives in the organisation of the synodal life of the Church. Thus was formed the pentarchy: Rome, Constantinople, Alexandria, Antioch and Jerusalem, even if in the course of history there have appeared outside the pentarchy other archbishops, metropolitans, primates and patriarchs.

(53) The synodal character of episcopal activity showed itself above all in questions under discussion which interested several local churches or the churches as a whole. Thus, in each region, different types of synods or councils, local or regional, and conferences of bishops were organised. Their forms could change

85

according to different places and times, their guiding principle, nevertheless, being to manifest and make efficacious the life of the Church by joint action of the bishops, under the presidency of the one whom they recognised as the first among them. In fact, according to canon 34 of the apostles, belonging to the canonical tradition of our Churches, the first among the bishops takes a decision only in agreement with the other bishops and the latter decide nothing of importance without the agreement of the first.

(54) In ecumenical councils, convened in the Holy Spirit at times of crisis, the bishops of the Church, with supreme authority, decided together about faith and issued canons to affirm the tradition of the apostles in historical circumstances which directly threatened the faith, unity and sanctifying work of the whole people of God, putting at risk the very existence of the Church and its fidelity to its Founder, Jesus Christ.

(55) It is in this perspective of communion among local churches that an approach could be made to the question of primacy in the Church in general and, in particular, to that of the primacy of the Bishop of Rome, which constitutes a serious divergence between us and which will be discussed in the future.

Parish Papers

The Prayer of the Heart:
East and West
*Sister Pamela Hayes, RSCJ**

The Prayer of the Heart is familiar to most of us in the West as the Jesus Prayer of the Eastern Orthodox tradition, with its repetition of the phrase, 'Lord Jesus Christ, Son of God, have mercy on me a sinner'. But the matrix of the tradition goes back, beyond the divisions of East and West, to the early Fathers of the Church and the New Testament teaching itself on prayer.

The New Testament

The early Fathers explored ways both of taking literally the injuncion to 'pray always', 'without ceasing' (1Thess 5:17 and Lk 18:1), and of realising how it applied to the innermost response to God in every aspect of a human life. In the Sermon on the Mount, Matthew's Jesus emphasises that what counts above all in prayer is simplicity and sincerity, with the words: 'Go into your inner room and pray to your Father in secret', and 'do not use many words... Your Father knows what you need' (Mt 6:6-8). Then, the Jesus of the Fourth Gospel encourages prayer in his name, as he tells his disciples that if we 'ask anything in his name, it will be given by the Father' (Jn 16:23,24). Finally, St Paul makes it clear that it is the Spirit who empowers all our prayer because 'we do not know

---

* See pp.169-170 for details of Contributors.

how to pray as we should, but the Spirit prays for us' (Rom 8:26), and 'No one can say "Jesus is Lord" except by the power of the Holy Spirit' (1Cor 12:3).

The New Testament, therefore, already provides the foundation for a tradition of prayer that can be uttered in a few words, sounding from the deep inner space of the human heart, in the power of the Spirit, who makes it possible for us to pray in the name of Jesus to God our Father. It can, moreover, be a prayer so hidden and so part of our inner being that it can be continuous, as continuous as breathing.

The early Fathers of the Church developed this tradition, always emphasising the need for a realism that integrates prayer and life. There was to be no divorce of prayer from everyday life. In their language, prayer had to move, with the inner dynamism of the Word of God, from the mind to the heart, and thence to engage the whole person's life-style. '*Theoria*' and '*praxis*' went inexorably together. Certain key personalities allow us to highlight this development of teaching in the Church from the fourth to the fifteenth centuries.

John Cassian

In the fourth century, John Cassian, generally believed to be a Scythian, which would account for his fluency in both Greek and Latin, is particularly appropriate for our consideration because his spiritual search took him from East to West. Cassian began his journey in the monasteries of Palestine, in Bethlehem, but went in search of spiritual teaching in the deserts of Egypt and finally brought what he had learnt, in teaching and experience, to Marseilles and the Provençal region of Southern France, where he made a monastic foundation for the West.

In the now famous *Conferences* 9 and 10, Cassian[1] speaks of the formation of the mind by the Word of God as the bedrock foundation of all Christian prayer. He sees our human experience being challenged and encouraged by a contemplative reflection upon the Word of God in Scripture. This is the monastic tradition known as *Lectio Divina*: the Latin for pondering on the Word of God which, like a mirror, will reflect my life back to me. Such ruminating on the Word of God in Scripture is the way in which most of us in the Western tradition of spirituality have understood the term 'meditation'. Those who have given themselves to its practice know by experience that such reflection on Christ in the Word of God does, in fact, provide a mirror in which they can see the potential fulness of the life to which we are all called. They know, too, that as they grow in their spiritual journey, both prayer and life simplify. They need fewer and fewer words, and they can rest in the stillness of one word, savouring its meaning deep within.

This, in fact, is the natural progression to the teaching on another kind of meditation which Cassian gave to those who were ready for it. This he called 'secret meditation', in a manner reminiscent of the words in Matthew's Gospel about praying in secret (Mt 6:6), the secret place being the heart. This kind of meditation always presupposed the other as its natural foundation: the process of becoming familiar with the Word of God in Scripture. In practice, secret meditation meant the repetition of a treasured word or phrase of Scripture so that it could, quite literally, be learnt by heart, not by dint of mental effort but as a consequence of the reverent familiarity of the lover.

Our modern world of advertisement knows only too well the power of repetition. We know about brands of consumer goods not because we have exercised our minds on the subject, but because we see and hear the words repeated constantly: so we know them *by heart*. This psychological truth was known to Cassian by experience in the spiritual life, as he also knew well the inability of the human mind and imagination to rest and be still with any ease. But he was also aware that, if any lasting life transformation was to take place, the Word of God must penetrate from the mind to the heart, that is, from the level of intellectual understanding to the deepest level of human experience, integrating thought and feeling with spiritual intuition. Only in this way could the whole human personality be transformed in the practice of an everyday life-style.

The purpose of Cassian's teaching about repetition was to still the mind from discursive thought during the time given to prayer and to take the Word from the mind to the core and centre of the whole being that we call the heart. This, it was believed, would lead to an ever deeper stillness and silence in the time of prayer and a growing freedom of spirit in everyday life, as the wisdom of God's will became incresingly its guiding star. Such repetition might begin vocally, but, with faithful practice, it could become simply an inner repetition, in reality, a listening to the Word in the depths of the heart: the 'inner room' or 'secret place' of the Gospel. In modern language, this is the real meaning and purpose of Cassian's teaching on purity of heart. Cassian spoke of the graced fruit of such a practice in terms of God's gift of the 'prayer of fire': peak moments, God-given, of longing love and resting in the fire of God's love.

Cassian's own word-phrase was: 'God come to my

aid. Lord make haste to help me.' It was intended that the choice of a phrase should be free according to the Spirit's inspiration of each person. But, gradually, usually under the influence of an inspired teacher, a certain phrase became fixed for common use, and tended to focus on the holy name.

Diadochus of Photike

It was, however, Diadochus of Photike in the fifth century who really moved the point of focus on to the holy name, although not as a fixed formula, thus, even at this early date, unconsciously forging links with the mystical trends of other, non-Christian religions. This he did together with an attempt to explain the psychological value of the process involved in such a practice of prayer. Diadochus emphasised that the memory, in particular the memory of God, held the key to the transformation of life through the integration and unity of the whole person. He believed that if we could remember the presence, the power and the love of God, we would see our lives reformed and transformed. Being practical, he realised that memory and remembering imply repetition: more specifically, the repetition of one short phrase that would unify human consciousness and heal the psyche by unifying mind and heart, and so our life.

Such teaching, looked at from the vantage point of our psychologically conscious age, with its interest in unity consciousness, in both religious and secular spheres, has a strangely familiar and modern ring, without attempting to put concepts that belong to the twentieth century into the mind of Diadochus. His practical advice, after more complex attempts to explain his reasons, was simple. 'Whoever wishes to purify his heart should set it afire with the continual memory of the Lord Jesus, taking this alone for his meditation.'[2] It was in this way that the practice of remembering God became more and more linked with the repetition of the name of Jesus, the name which means Saviour, the one who is our healing. The name gathered together in one all that seemed essential in the movement of prayer. It united both adoration and compunction, the most reverent and loving awareness of God together with the most penetrating experience of God's forgiving and healing love.

The Hesychasts

In the seventh century, John Climacus, speaking for the Hesychasts, who both preached and practised this prayer in stillness and tranquillity, as the word 'Hesychast' implies, articulated another dimension to the teaching on this Prayer of the heart. '*Hesychia* is a continual adoration of the ever-present God. Let the memory of Jesus be united to your breath, and then you will know the benefit of *hesychia*.'[3] This psycho-physical linking of the repetition of the name of Jesus to the rhythm of breathing, developed by the monks of Mount Athos and Mount Sinai within the Eastern Orthodox tradition of Hesychasm, was popularised in the fourteenth century. While the Hesychasts found their most famous advocate and theologian in Gregory Palamas, who spoke with deep appreciation about the whole tradition of the Prayer of the Heart, he considered this aspect with moderating discretion. But used wisely, he considered it as a truly holistic way of praying, appropriate to any believer in Christianity's most central mystery of the Incarnation.[4]

England

It was in the same fourteenth century that the West, indeed England, gave evidence of a form of prayer that echoes the Eastern Prayer of the Heart, in the work of the anonymous author of *The Cloud of Unknowing*. The essence of this prayer is a 'naked intent' and a 'blind stirring of love', reaching out to God hidden in a 'cloud of unknowing'. All thoughts of the mind are to be placed under a 'cloud of forgetting' in the time of this prayer. To aid in this stilling of the mind, it was suggested that one word be repeated as a support to a wordless reaching out to God from the heart.

'Lift up your heart by a humble impulse of love...a simple reaching out directly towards God is sufficient... If you like, you can have this reaching out wrapped up and enfolded in a single word...such as God or love. Fasten this word to your heart so that whatever happens it will never go away... With this word you are to beat upon this cloud...and to strike down every kind of thought under a cloud of forgetting.'[5]

Russia

It was, however, nineteenth century Russia and the neighbouring Slav countries that really popularised the Prayer of the Heart, with the fully developed form of the Jesus Prayer, through the compilation of the teachings of the Fathers of the Church in the great resource work of the *Philokalia*.[6] It was further popularised by *The Way of the Pilgrim*,[7] which is still a best-seller today.

The title itself suggests a further dimension in the use of the Prayer of the Heart. The emphasis was no longer only upon a time of stillness given to the practice of this way of prayer. Instead, the practice was expected to spill over actively in a kind of ejaculatory prayer that accompanied life's journey, whatever had to be done and wherever a person went. The pilgrim wandering from place to place became a model of all life's seeking after God, in everything that happens.

Such a process of prayer, simple in word and sincere in intent, removed any sense of dichotomy between prayer and life, and was available to the learned and the unlettered alike. Prayer was really at the heart of life. It was experienced as the inner dimension of all relationships and all activity. Life was the lived out expression of that tension of longing and reaching out for God in the desire of the heart that is prayer.

A Way for Today

Such a way of prayer remains highly relevant to our needs today. It is, perhaps, almost a truism to say that the most effective ecumenical dialogue in the contemporary world is that which is achieved through a communion of silent prayer. Words that attempt to explain can so often divide, but meeting together in a silence open to God at the heart of all reality can only draw us into the unity that Christ prayed would be ours at His last supper (Jn 17).

It is a way of prayer that can lead us very simply into stillness, integrating mind and heart and body as we become more aware of the presence of the Blessed Trinity within us. This, in fact, is the glorious mystery of the Prayer of the Heart. It is, in reality, not dependent upon our own prayer. We simply become present to the relations of the Blessed Trinity in our tending to become more centred, which is really the deepest meaning of 'concentration'.

Jesus, the Son of God, prays in us and for us, as we are reminded by the word we utter. He is the Word uttered in the Godhead, through whom all things came into being. We pray, quite literally, in His name, in the power and breath of the Spirit, who is the love bonding us in Christ to the Father, our God, to whom we pray. It is this reality of adoration that reminds us of the words of Jesus to the Samaritan woman in the Fourth Gospel: 'The hour is coming, and now is, when true worshippers will adore the Father in spirit and in truth.' (Jn 4:23) Understanding these words in their spiritual sense, we can see that all real adoration of the Father can only be in the power of the Holy Spirit, made possible through the Truth that is Jesus, the Christ, the Son of God.[8]

The Gift of the Spirit

All such Trinitarian prayer becomes possible because of the promise of Jesus. 'If anyone thirst, let him come to me and drink, the one who believes in me... From within him will flow rivers of living water.' 'Now this', says the Evangelist, 'he said of the Spirit' who was to be received after Jesus was glorified in his death and resurrection (Jn 7:37-39). The living water was the symbol of the gift of the Spirit who prays for us in Christ to Abba, our Father (Rom 8:15). However, there is an interesting nuance in this text which allows for two interpretations, depending upon the punctuation in the original Greek text. Richness of spiritual meaning, always present in the Fourth Gospel, suggests that we take both meanings in turn, because they underline a double truth that is highly relevant to our spiritual growth, as well as to the East-West ecumenical dialogue that is our particular concern here.

According to one sense, the gift of the Spirit, the living water, will flow from the heart of the believer. Here is the source of the Prayer of the Heart, as we have been reflecting upon its development over the centuries, especially in the context of the Eastern tradition. But, equally, we may take the sense to mean that the gift of the Spirit, living water, will flow from the heart of Christ, after his glorification. John 19:34-37, which sees blood and water flowing from the pierced side of Jesus on the cross, points to the fulfilment both of the promise of Jesus concerning the living water (Jn 7:37-39) and of the prophecy of Zechariah: 'They shall look upon Him whom they have pierced' (12:10).

Such interpretations, far from being mutually exclusive, are complementary: ambivalent rather than ambiguous. They convey the deep spiritual insight that it is by the releasing of the Spirit, through the pierced side of Christ, that those who believe are enabled to live, from within their own inner depths, a new life in the Spirit of Christ. They point to the interiorising process of becoming other Christs, going beyond simply looking at Jesus the Christ, which is the ultimate purpose of the mystery of the Incarnation.

It would seem, therefore, that the long tradition of the Prayer of the Heart in the East and the discreet interiorising of the truth symbolised by the Sacred Heart pierced on the cross of glory in the West, meet in the richness of these texts of St John's Gospel. They draw us into the simple practice of a Prayer of the

Heart that could make us, Christians of both the East and the West, one in the heart of Christ.

A Way for Us

We have only to begin here and now. We can pray the Jesus Prayer as we know it in the now traditional formula, or we can use another word or phrase which, in essence, is the same kind of prayer in the holy name. The Aramaic '*Maranatha*', meaning 'Come, Lord' (1 Cor 16:22) was the word given by John Main, a twentieth century teacher of the tradition.[9] St Ignatius of Loyola gave yet another variant of this kind of prayer in his second and third methods of prayer in *The Spiritual Exercises*,[10] generally less well known than the 'Ignatian Contemplation'. We can, very gently, without any exaggeration, link our prayer with the rhythm of our breathing, breathing in with the name 'Jesus' and out with the name 'Abba', letting our very breath remind us of the breath of the Holy Spirit. Greek, Latin and Hebrew have the same word for spirit and breath. This is surely Trinitarian prayer. Or, we may have our own variant. The exact words matter little. We just need to keep the process simple and sincere, praying faithfully and in stillness at the times we have decided to give to this prayer; and then using it, if we wish, as a help in all our needs, for serenity and patience as we go about our pilgrim way, doing whatever we need to do in each present moment. But there must be no pressure or anxiety in the way we use these words. They are simply there as a support, a sort of pilgrim staff, as we go on our way being a pilgrim in our heart, always seeking God wherever He is to be found.

For still the truth remains: we know that God can be found in the heart of everyone and everything. He need not remain hidden to the eye of the heart, the eye of faith, if we seek Him with all our heart. But when all is said and done about the ways that we may choose, there remains a short cut to this prayer of the heart. It is a way not usually chosen because it is the way of suffering, that entails the wounding of the heart. However, the opportunity comes to all of us at some time. If we take it, we shall know this truth by experience, painfully but gratefully. At this moment we may, with our Western tradition, look upon the pierced and open Sacred Heart of Christ and allow ourselves to be called within, to our own centre, in an ever-deepening form of a Prayer of the Heart that is the heritage of the Eastern tradition of Christianity.

NOTES

1   John Cassian, *Conferences* (Colm Luibheid, ed.; Classics of Western Spirituality; Paulist Press: New York/Ramsey, 1985).
2   Diadochus of Photike, *On Spiritual Knowledge,* no. 97, in *The Philokalia,* trans. G.E.H. Palmer, Philip Sherrard and Kallistos Ware, vol. I (Faber and Faber: London/Boston, 1979). Cf Irenée Hausherr, *The Name of Jesus* (Cistercian Publications: Kalamazoo, 1978), pp. 220-229.
3   John Climacus, quotation in Hausherr, *The Name of Jesus,* p. 281.
4   Cf John Meyendorff, *A Study of Gregory Palamas* (St Vladimir's Seminary Press: Crestwood, 1974); *Byzantine Theology* (St Vladimir's Seminary Press: Crestwood, 1974).
5   James Walsh SJ (ed.), *The Cloud of Unknowing* (Classics of Western Spirituality; Paulist Press: New York/Ramsey, 1984), Chapter 7.
6   E. Kadloubovsky and G.E.H.Palmer (trans.), *Writings from the Philokalia on the Prayer of the Heart* (Faber and Faber: London, 1951).
7. R.M.French, *The Way of the Pilgrim* (SPCK: London, 1972).
8   Cf Gabriel Bunge, 'The "Spiritual Prayer": on the Trinitarian Mysticism of Evagrius of Pontus', *Monastic Studies,* 17 (Christmas, 1986).
9   Cf John Main, *Word into Silence* (Darton, Longman and Todd: London, 1988).
10 Louis J. Puhl (ed.), *The Spiritual Exercises of St Ignatius* (Loyola University Press: Chicago, 1951).

How Two Worlds Drifted Apart
*Canon Hugh Wybrew**

In any family, children born to the same parents may turn out to be quite different in character and temperament. They may grow up to have apparently little in common. If they go to different schools, and then make their lives in different surroundings, they may well end up having little to do with one another. Not infrequently a quarrel over the family inheritance finally sours family relationships and brings all contacts to an end.

That may serve as a passable analogy for what happened to relationships between the two dominant members of the Christian family, the Greek East and the Latin West. The Great Schism, as it is often called, between Constantinople and Rome, is traditionally dated 1054. It was probably the most significant of all the divisions which have afflicted Christianity, though it was not the first. Its roots go far back into the early centuries of the Christian movement.

East and West in the Roman Empire

Christianity began as a sect of Judaism in the Eastern part of the Roman Empire. Beginning from Jerusalem in Judaea, faith in Jesus as the crucified and risen Messiah spread rapidly throughout the Roman world and was soon established in Rome itself, the capital of the Empire. The Roman Empire was a political unity,

---

* See pp.169-170 for details of Contributors.

but it held together a wide variety of peoples and cultures. It included North Africa, Egypt, the Middle East, Asia Minor, the Balkans, Italy, France, Spain and Portugal, and North-West Europe. In the Middle East it included the Syrians, with their own distinctive language and culture, and the Copts in Egypt with theirs. The dominant language in the East was Greek, the common language of all educated people in the lands which had formed part of Alexander the Great's empire towards the end of the fourth century before Christ. Hellenistic culture dominated the cities, even if indigenous cultures remained strong in rural areas in the East.

Latin was the official language of the whole Empire for purposes of government, administration and law, and it was the common language of educated people in the West. One of the sources of the separation of Christians in communion with Rome from those in communion with Constantinople is the distinction between these two linguistic and cultural traditions within the Roman Empire. The mentality of those who thought and wrote in Greek was different from that of those who thought and wrote in Latin.

Generalisations are always in need of qualification; but it is not too misleading to say that the Greek mind was more inclined to philosophy and intellectual speculation than the Latin, while the Latins had a definite bent for political organisation and the administration of law, and were less given to philosophical discussion. There is sufficient truth in the distinction between Greek East and Latin West to make the contrast a valid one. Among educated people there were, of course, those who knew both languages. Perhaps it was the case that more Greek speakers knew Latin than the other way round. But different languages are always a problem for communication and mutual understanding, and so it was among Christians formed in different linguistic and cultural traditions. It was not always easy to translate theological terms from Greek into Latin and vice versa, for words apparently equivalent often had different resonances.

There were other contrasts between the Eastern and Western parts of the Roman Empire which contributed to the ultimate divergence of the churches there. The Hellenistic world of the East was a world of many cities, centres of Graeco-Roman civilisation. Each city had its own bishop. The East had four great centres of Christianity. Alexandria and Antioch, where the disciples were first called Christians, were both apostolic sees, claiming foundation by Mark and Peter, respectively. They were important from earliest times and each of them became the home of influential theological schools. Constantinople, the New Rome, sprang into almost immediate ecclesiastical significance when it became the capital of the Empire in 330 AD. In 381, its bishop was recognised as second only to the bishop of Rome and, in 451, he was given wider jurisdiction, in spite of the protests of the bishop of Rome. Constantinople also claimed apostolic origin in the missionary work of Andrew. In 451, too, Jerusalem was accorded recognition as a major Christian centre, possessing and guarding the holy places connected with the earthly life of Christ and looking back to James the brother of the Lord as its first bishop. By the sixth century, the bishops of all four sees came to be called Patriarchs; and the Patriarch of Constantinople further styled himself 'Ecumenical' Patriarch, as bishop of the capital city of the whole inhabited world.

Apart from Italy and North Africa, the West was less urbanised. Its dioceses were far larger and largely rural. Though there were other important Christian centres, such as Arles in Gaul and Carthage in North Africa, there was none with the same claims to pre-eminence as Rome. The West had only one Patriarchate and after the Arab Muslim conquest of North Africa, early in the seventh century, no church was left which might claim any kind of independence of Rome.

Theological Controversy

The Greek and Latin mentalities were reflected in different approaches to theological issues. The Greek, Eastern, Christian mind was perhaps more adventurous intellectually. Almost all the doctrinal controversies which rent the early Church were of Eastern origin. Educated Christians tried to explain and commend their faith in terms of contemporary philosophy. This may have been necessary but could be dangerous.

The first of the major doctrinal controversies, Arianism, began early in the fourth century and more or less coincided with Constantines's recognition of Christianity. Arius maintained that the Son was not equal with the Father. He was, rather, the highest of the creatures made by the Father, created out of nothing to be then the Father's agent in the rest of creation. This affirmation provoked a major crisis in the Church, affecting not only theologians but the Christian in the street. Constantine had backed Christianity as the religion most likely to be of service in uniting his multicultural empire: he did not want the unifying force itself divided. It was the emperor who called the bishops of the Empire together at Nicea in 325 to resolve the issue. The majority of participants were Eastern bishops. They adopted the famous term 'homoousios', of one substance, to define the relationship of the Son to the Father. Championed especially by the deacon Athanasius from Alexandria, this word was included in the creed put out by the Council, the first of the 'Ecumenical' Councils.

Arian teaching remained influential, however, and it was not until 381 that the second Ecumenical Council of Constantinople finally united most Christians on the basis of the faith of Nicea and proclaimed the Holy Spirit as the third co-equal and co-eternal Person of the Holy Trinity. There seems to have been no Western participation in this Council at all, though its decisions were fully acceptable to the West so far as they concerned matters of faith.

Controversy moved on from Trinitarian theology to Christology, the doctrine of the person of Jesus Christ. The theological schools of Alexandria and Antioch thought and spoke of the relationship between the divine and human natures in Jesus in different ways. Nestorius, bishop of Constantinople from 428 to 431, was an Antiochene. As such, he preferred to think of there being two persons, one human and one divine, in the incarnate Jesus Christ. He was bitterly opposed by Cyril, bishop of Alexandria, not only on doctrinal but also on ecclesiastical grounds, for Cyril deeply resented the upstart claims of Constantinople to second place in the hierarchy of sees. Nestorius would only speak of Mary as Mother of Christ. Cyril insisted that she was Mother of God – *Theotokos* – since he to whom she gave birth was none other than the Second Person of the Trinity become a human being in her womb. The third Ecumenical Council of Ephesus in 431 upheld the teaching of Cyril.

But the more extreme exponents of Alexandrian theology went too far in the direction opposed to that of Nestorius, and in the person of Eutyches, a monk of Constantinople, virtually denied the real humanity of the incarnate Christ. The fourth Ecumenical Council of Chalcedon, in 451, met to resolve the issue of how the two natures should be conceived as united in the one person of Jesus Christ and, condemning both Nestorius and Eutyches, proclaimed Jesus Christ to be one Person, in whom the two natures, human and divine, are united 'unconfusedly, unchangeably, indivisibly, inseparably'.

However, the Chalcedonian definition was not acceptable to all Christians in the East. Continuing doctrinal disagreement became embittered by the attempts of the imperial authorities to enforce agreement, often on the basis of compromise; and, by the end of the sixth century, a family of Eastern Churches, the Armenian, Syrian, Coptic and Ethiopian Churches, had detached themselves from the Chalcedonian orthodox Church of the Empire, and constituted a group of Churches called 'monophysite' by their opponents, since they preferred to speak of only 'one nature of God the Word incarnate'. The Nestorians had rejected Ephesus, and untimately formed themselves into the Church of the East, nowadays often known as the Assyrian Church, with its centre in Persia, safely outside the Empire.

Christological controversies continued for another three centuries or more and three more Ecumenical Councils were held, in 533, 680/1 and 787, before they were finally laid to rest. Much of the controversy was focused on attempts to reconcile the monophysite party, sponsored by the imperial government. These theological compromises , as they were seen in the West, were strongly opposed by Rome which, theologically less adventurous, was usually on the side of orthodox tradition, except in the case of Pope Honorius in the early seventh century, who espoused the cause of monothelitism, the doctrine that, although there were two natures in the incarnate Christ, there was only one – divine – will. He and it were condemned at the sixth Ecumenical Council of Constantinople in 680/1.

Schisms and Status

Since there were periods, sometimes lengthy, when views ultimately condemned as heretical were prevalent in Constantinople, both in Church and State, relations between Constantinople and Rome were a good deal strained. There were temporary schisms, such as the so-called Acacian schism from 482 to 518, which was provoked by the attempt of the Emperor Zeno to unite monophysites and Chalcedonian orthodox. Zeno promoted the Henotikon, the document drawn up, it seems, by the Patriarch Acacius of Constantinople, which sought to effect reconciliation by declining to address the issue of how many natures there were in the incarnate Christ. Widely accepted in the East, it was firmly rejected by Rome, when it was issued in 482, as making too many concessions to the monophysites.

Although Rome and Constantinople were reconciled in 518, when a new Emperor, Justin, came to the throne, relations became severely strained again under his nephew Justinian. Justinian continued the imperial policy of trying to unite monophysites and Chalcedonians, and hoped to placate the former by condemning writings of Theodore of Mopsuestia, Theodoret of Cyrus and Ibas of Edessa, three Antiochene theologians particularly disliked by the monophysites as, in their view, tainted with Nestorianism. In 551, the Emperor decreed the condemnation of the so-called Three Chapters. Pope Vigilius excommunicated those Eastern bishops who accepted the decision. The fifth Ecumenical Council of 553 was called to settle the dispute. Vigilius at first refused to consent to imperial policy, but finally gave way to considerable pressure.

In the following century, another attempt at theological reconciliation between monophysites and Chalcedonians caused further dispute between East and West. The Emperor Heraclius took up the doctrine that, though there were two natures in Christ, there was only one 'energy', that of the divine Word. Formulated by Sergius, Patriarch of Constantinople, it achieved much success in reconciling the monophysites. It was rashly espoused by Pope Honorius, who wrote to Sergius of one will in Christ. This doctrine, known as monothelitism, was embodied in the Ecthesis put out by the Emperor Heraclius in 638. It was repeatedly condemned by successive Popes until the sixth Ecumenical Council in 680/1 repudiated it, and anathematised Honorius.

These disputes and consequent breaches in communion helped to foster a certain mistrust between Rome and Constantinople. Relations were not improved by the growing claims of Rome to supreme authority in the whole Church, East and West. From very early times, the church in Rome had been accorded a certain pre-eminence: it was the church which 'presided in love' over all the churches. But there was a subtle shift in the fifth century in the nature of the claims made by Rome.

Pope Leo the Great, bishop of Rome from 440 to 461, worked hard to advance and strengthen Roman claims to jurisdiction throughout the West and would have liked to extend his influence in the East as well. Doctrinally, Leo made an important contribution to the outcome of the Council of Chalcedon. But his claims for Roman jurisdiction, based on the apostolic foundation of the church in Rome and on the position given to Peter in the New Testament, were never recognised in the East. Leo opposed Chalcedon's recognition of Constantinople's jurisdiction in the East and of its status as second only to Rome, alleging the rights of the ancient patriarchates in the East.

As Roman claims developed, the East evolved its own understanding of the Church as governed by the Pentarchy: the five Patriarchates of Rome, Constantinople, Alexandria, Antioch and Jerusalem. Gradually, incompatible doctrines of the Church were emerging in East and West.

Political Division

Political tensions were gradually added to those ecclesiastical. From the end of the fourth century, the Roman Empire was ruled by two Emperors, one in the East, the other in the West. Throughout the fifth century, the Western part of the Empire was increasingly weakened by barbarian invasions and it finally came to an end in 476. The barbarian rulers sometimes maintained relations with Constantinople, and Rome continued to look to the Empire in the East for support. But the bishops of Rome were, in practice, usually obliged to take independent action to ensure the life of the city: its water supplies, even its defence against barbarian attack, became the responsibility of the popes, who also conducted negotiations with barbarian leaders.

In the sixth century, Justinian recovered Rome and Italy for the Empire, as well as North Africa. But by the end of the century they had been lost for good and, by 640, North Africa, Egypt and much of the Middle East had become part of the new Muslim Arab Empire ruled first from Damascus and later from Baghdad. It was the turn of the Empire in the East to come under pressure from a rival political force, which was to press upon the Roman Empire and gradually erode it, until its final collapse in 1453.

By the mid-eighth century, the popes had lost hope of getting effective support from Constantinople. Another doctrinal controversy, over the legitimacy of making and venerating icons, had broken out in the East, when in 726 the Emperor Leo III ordered the destruction of all images as idolatrous. Promoted by a succession of emperors, iconoclasm was strongly resisted by Church leaders and, in particular, by the monks. The popes supported the defenders of the icons, so straining relations with the Empire. In 787, the seventh Ecumenical Council approved the use of icons and their veneration and, though a second period of iconoclasm followed, the final victory of the icons was achieved in 843.

Meanwhile, Rome had turned Westwards to make an alliance with the new Frankish Empire and, in 800, Charlemagne was crowned Holy Roman Emperor in Rome by Pope Leo III. The concept of a single Christian Empire ruled by one Emperor had been fatally undermined and the creation of a Western Empire laying claim to divine authority over against the Eastern Empire prepared the way for the final separation of the Church in the Western from the Church in the Eastern Roman Empire. That Empire, now usually called Byzantine, was by this time a Greek Empire.

The now politically independent West was definitely Latin.

Two Churches

The Church in the Byzantine Empire, too, was now definitely Greek: the non-Greek populations had been largely lost after the Arab conquest in the early seventh century. It would not be too anachronistic to speak now of the Orthodox and Roman Catholic Churches. They were still in communion with one another, but they were growing apart. They followed different liturgical customs, they had developed different styles of Church architecture and decoration. They were beginning to clash over one serious doctrinal difference, the use of the *'filioque'* in the Nicene Creed.

In that creed, put out in 381 by the Council of Constantinople, the Holy Spirit was said to proceed from the Father. Towards the end of the sixth century, the Church in Spain began to add 'and from the Son' – *'filioque'* in Latin – to the creed. It is usually said to have been an anti-Arian gesture, emphasising the equality of the Son with the Father. From Spain it spread to Gaul and, from about 800, was generally used in the Church in the Frankish Empire. When Frankish monks recited the creed with the *filioque* in their monastery on the Mount of Olives in Jerusalem, objection was raised by the Eastern monks. In 867, Patriarch Photius of Constantinople expounded his objections to the *filioque* in a letter. The issue was one among others in a complex situation in which Rome was involved with rival Patriarchs in Constantinople and which produced another temporary schism. Fresh tensions arose from the confrontation of Latin and Greek missionaries in Bulgaria and Moravia.

By the tenth century, the two parts of the Church were set on divergent courses, teased apart by doctrinal differences, ecclesiastical and secular politics, and cultural differences. A head-on clash occurred in 1054. Though usually referred to as the 'Great Schism', the importance of the mutual excommunication of the Patriarch of Constantinople, Michael Cerularius, and the papal legates led by Cardinal Humbert, sent by Pope Leo IX, has been exaggerated. The Latins demanded that the Patriarch give up the title 'Ecumenical' and recognise the *filioque*. He naturally refused. The excommunications were personal and discussions continued in an effort to restore harmony. But relations had been still further soured and strained.

The Crusades finally put an end to any hope of reconciliation between Eastern and Western Christianity. The first Crusade captured Jerusalem in 1099. The Latins slaughtered local Orthodox and other Christians as well as Jews and Muslims. A Latin Patriarch was installed and the Latins took control of the Holy Places. The situation of Eastern Christians under Islamic rule was worsened, since the Muslims now came to associate all Christians with European invasion and domination. All the crusaders passed through Byzantine territory and caused much anxiety to the Emperors in Constantinople. It was the fourth Crusade which, in 1204, captured and sacked Constantinople itself, the capital of the Christian Empire, and set up a Latin Empire and Latin Patriarchate. The Greeks recaptured the city in 1261. But the Greek Orthodox never forgave the Catholic Latins and the Greek Empire was fatally weakened.

Attempts at Reconciliation

Popular hostility to the West was such that the two attempts subsequently made to reconcile the two Churches were doomed to failure. At the Council of Lyons in 1274, and at that of Florence in 1439, the Empire, desperate for Western military help against Muslim pressure, was ready to make doctrinal concessions and recognize the authority of Rome. A union was agreed in 1274, but had fizzled out by 1289. By 1439, the Empire was reduced to little more than the city of Constantinople and the Turks were at the door. Again, a union was agreed. But opposition in Constantinople and in Russia rendered it ineffective. No Western help was given and, in 1453, Constantinople fell.

Both unions had been signed more under the pressure of political necessity on the Eastern side than from genuine theological agreement. During the Middle Ages, the two theological traditions diverged still more, the East conserving the Greek patristic tradition, the West following Augustine and then the massive synthesis constructed by Thomas Aquinas using Aristotelian philosophy. After 1453, most of the Orthodox Churches were under Muslim rule and largely cut off from the intellectual movements which helped to shape the Western Christian tradition – the Renaissance, the Reformation, and later the Enlightenment. In Russia, too, where the Orthodox Church was closely allied with the State, there was a strong tendency to close the frontiers against Western European influences. Each of the two Churches came to think of the other as schismatic and heretical.

But not all links had been finally broken. In some places, such as Cyprus and the Greek islands, Orthodox and Roman Catholics lived alongside each other, even worshipping in different parts of the same church building, and they sometimes received communion together, up to the early part of the eighteenth century. For some time before then, Roman Catholic missionaries had been active in various parts of the East, establishing contacts with the Eastern Churches. They were also trying to persuade them to recognize the authority of Rome and were successful to the extent of persuading some groups of Christians in all the Eastern Churches to enter into communion with the Pope.

So came into being the so-called Uniate Churches, keeping their own rites and customs, but submitting to Roman authority and, of course, accepting Roman Catholic doctrine. By the Union of Brest-Litovsk, in 1595, many Orthodox Christians in the Ukraine entered into communion with Rome, together with other groups similarly under Lithuanian or Polish political control. In 1701, many Romanian Orthodox in Transylvania, then under Austrian rule, did the same. In 1724 there was a split in the Orthodox Patriarchate of Antioch, resulting in the formation of a Uniate Church, called Melkite, in the territories of the Patriarchates of Antioch, Jerusalem and Alexandria.

These and other smaller churches, which entailed the religious division of peoples hitherto sustained under difficult circumstances in their sense of ethnic identity by their common faith, caused immense resentment against Rome on the part of the Orthodox Churches, which felt that their weakness had been exploited by Rome for its own ends. Their creation added another chapter to the story of the violence done by the Catholic West to the Orthodox East. Any lingering state of communion between the two Churches had come to an end by the middle of the eighteenth century.

To the Present

So the two sister Churches came to be no longer on speaking terms. Each claimed the whole of the family inheritance – that is, to be the one, holy, catholic and apostolic Church of the creed. The dogmatic additions made to that inheritance by the Roman Catholic Church in the nineteenth and twentieth centuries – the Immaculate Conception, Papal Infallibility and the Assumption – have added to the list of doctrinal differences.

The lifting of the anathemas of 1054 by Pope Paul VI and the Ecumenical Patriarch Athenagoras I in 1965 symbolised a shift in relations. But suspicion of Rome among Orthodox Christians is still deeply rooted and the legacy of a thousand years of conflict will take a long time to overcome. Memories must be healed and inherited attitudes changed before the love which Christ commanded his disciples to have for one another can unite in one communion Churches which have developed in separation and lived in mutual hostility for so long. We can be thankful for the beginning of that process of healing and reconciliation.

Regaining our Lost Unity
*Father Paul McPartlan**

Introduction

1967 was a memorable year, not least at sea. Francis
Chichester sailed single-handed around the world, the
Torrey Canyon ran aground and the QE2 was launched.
It was, indeed, a year marked by conflict, as in the
Middle East six-day war, but it ended on a distinct
note of hope, with the first successful human heart
transplant.

There were other notes of hope, too, sounded not
least in Rome and Constantinople (Istanbul). Pope
Paul VI decided formally to mark 1967 as the nineteen
hundredth anniversary of the martyrdom in Rome of
Saints Peter and Paul. At Easter, he wrote to the Ecumenical Patriarch, Athenagoras I, saying that he hoped
that this anniversary would be the occasion of 'a great
act of faith... on the part of the whole Church', because, said Pope Paul, 'we are convinced that what the
modern world needs first and foremost is faith, perhaps more than was ever so in the past'.[1] Patriarch
Athenagoras replied to the Pope saying that he was
personally sending a delegation to represent the Orthodox Church at the festal celebrations on June 29. In
a subsequent telegram of thanks for their participation,
Paul VI said to Athenagoras: 'May the kiss of peace
exchanged in the course of the liturgy be the harbinger
of the concelebration which will one day be the fruit

---

* See pp.169-170 for details of Contributors.

of the full unity which we so desire to see restored in complete fidelity to the Lord's will'.[2]

In fact, the following month, against all the rules of protocol,[3] Pope Paul announced that, in faith, charity, friendship and gratitude, he intended to make 'a fraternal and official visit to Patriarch Athenagoras' in Istanbul.[4] This he duly did on July 25. In October, Athenagoras wrote to Paul VI, saying: 'we have always had the desire to come to Rome and visit you in your venerable see as a further sign of our deep brotherly love and of the honour in which we hold you, and also to strengthen those fraternal relations between the holy Roman Catholic Church and our holy Orthodox Church which through the Lord's bounteous blessing have been freshly restored and are growing day by day'.[5]

This momentous year was duly crowned with the visit of Athenagoras to Rome at the end of October and with a joint declaration about moving towards unity, to which we shall return. Speaking in St Peter's, beside the Pope, Patriarch Athenagoras said the following rousing words.

'We stand in this holy place, at the side of Your Holiness, near the altar of sacrifice, preparing ourselves in heart and spirit for the future advance to a common Eucharist, and as we carry out in our souls the service of the washing of feet, we hear at this extraordinarily holy moment the blood of the Apostles Peter and Paul crying out, we hear the voice of the Church of the catacombs and of the martyrs of the Colosseum, and the voice of our common Fathers and teachers, calling on us to leave no ways and means untried to complete the holy work that has been begun – that of the perfect recomposition of the divided Church of Christ – so that the will of the Lord may be fulfilled, and the world may see the first mark of the Church according to our Creed, namely that she is 'One', shining forth brilliantly.'[6]

Nearly twenty five years on is an important time to take stock and ask how much nearer being truly One Catholics and Orthodox actually are. Recent difficulties in the dialogue have brought us to something of a cross-roads. My aim in this paper is to try and follow the instruction which God gave His people through the prophet Jeremiah.

'Halt at the cross-roads, look well, and ask yourselves which path it was that stood you in good stead long ago. That path follow, and you shall find rest for your souls.' (Jer 6:16)

Catholic Readiness

So let us note, first of all, the marked contrast between the ecumenical ardour of 1967 and the frosty aloofness of just a few years earlier. In 1951, another nineteen hundredth anniversary was being celebrated, namely that of St Paul's arrival in Greece. The Greek Orthodox Church invited representatives of all the Orthodox Churches to a solemn celebration of the anniversary. Spiridon, the Archbishop of Athens and all Greece, also invited the Catholic Church to participate. The Vatican's letter of reply said: 'The august pontiff, while he is grateful to Your Excellency for the invitation, regrets to find himself in the obligation of declining it'.[7] Rather ironically, the letter was signed, with due expressions of respect, by the then substitute at the Secretariat of State, Giovanni Battista Montini.

Clearly, on the Catholic side, nothing short of a revolution in attitudes occurred between 1951 and 1967. The watershed was the Second Vatican Council. The Council made very positive statements about what the Orthodox Church has and shares with the Catholic Church. In fact these statements, in the Council's *Decree on Ecumenism*, can now be seen as bearing the seeds of the three agreed statements which Catholic-Orthodox dialogue has subsequently produced.

Let us recall what the Council said about the Eastern Churches.

'Through the celebration of the Eucharist of the Lord in each of these Churches, the Church of God is built up and grows in stature.' (n.15)

The first agreed statement was subsequently about the Eucharist.

'These Churches, although separated from us, yet possess true sacraments, above all – by apostolic succession – the priesthood and the Eucharist, whereby they are still joined to us in closest intimacy.' (n.15)

The second statement duly dealt with the sacraments and the third was about the sacrament of Order and apostolic succession.

Looking forward to Catholic dialogue with these Churches, Vatican II gave an important directive.

'The Council urges all, but especially those who commit themselves to work for the restoration of the full communion that is desired between the Eastern Churches and the Catholic Church, to give due consideration to [the] special feature of the origin and growth of the Churches of the East and to the character of the relations which obtained between them and the Roman See before the separation and to form for themselves a correct evaluation of these facts. The careful observance of this will greatly contribute to the dialogue in view.' (no. 14)

In a remarkable manifestation of fraternity, 23 years later, in 1987, the Ecumenical Patriarch Dimitrios I was at the side of Pope John Paul II for the Liturgy of the Word at the start of Mass for the Second Sunday of Advent in St Peter's. Both preached and the Pope reaffirmed the attitude of the Council in the following words to the Patriarch.

'The Second Vatican Council asked that in the efforts to reestablish full communion with the Eastern Churches, particular consideration be given to "the character of the relations which obtained between them and the Roman See before the separation". These relations fully respected the power of those churches to "govern themselves according to their own disciplines". I wish to assure you, Your Holiness, that the See of Rome, so attentive to all that is involved in the tradition of the Church, wishes to respect fully this tradition of the Eastern Church.'[8]

Then they recited the Nicene-Constantinopolitan Creed in Greek *without* the *'filioque'*, thereby bringing a symbolic end to the dispute between East and West over that thorny issue.

The Catholic Church, then, is publicly committed to a unity with the Eastern Churches for which the ecclesial communion of the first millennium is the model (their separation being traditionally dated to 1054 AD). Following that model there would be no Roman appointment of Eastern bishops, for instance. Involvement with episcopal nomination pertains more to the local patriarch than to the primate and, though the pope is the universal *primate*, he is *patriarch* only of the West. Further exploration of the distinction between these two offices of the pope, as primate and patriarch, respectively, was urged over twenty years ago, in 1969, by Joseph Ratzinger.[9]

Orthodox Readiness

We have looked, so far, at the kindling of the official Catholic desire for unity, but it is already evident that the Orthodox Church was by no means a reluctant partner. In fact, one of the major initiatives which founded the modern ecumenical movement was taken by the Orthodox Church as long ago as 1920, when the Ecumenical Patriarchate issued an Encyclical Letter: 'Unto the Churches of Christ everywhere'.[10] In a most far-sighted way, the encyclical urged a rapprochement and fellowship (*'koinonia'* was the word used) between the Christian Churches. They should give up bitter estrangement and renew their love as relatives in the household of Christ, so as to favour what it called 'that blessed union which will be completed in the future in accordance with the will of God'.

In words which could equally have been written for our own day, the encyclical said that all the Churches are threatened alike by various modern dangers, such as 'the deification of wealth and the contempt of higher ideals', also 'the prevailing unchecked licentiousness', so there should be common study of these topics and cooperation in tackling them. It is sad to reflect, over seventy years later, when East and West are still celebrating separate Easters, that the first practical demonstration of 'a kindly disposition towards each other' suggested by the encyclical was 'the acceptance of a uniform calendar for the celebration of the great Christian feasts at the same time by all the Churches'. But let us be positive.

In 1963, the Pan-Orthodox Conference taking place on Rhodes accepted the initiative of the Ecumenical Patriarch Athenagoras and unanimously decided that 'our Eastern Orthodox Church suggests to the Roman Catholic Church the starting of a dialogue between the two Churches on an equal level'.[11] This suggestion was reiterated the following year, 1964, the same year as Vatican II's *Decree on Ecumenism*. So, under the inspiration of the Holy Spirit, there was a synchronised stirring in hearts on both sides.

Beginnings

Events moved swiftly. In 1965, both Churches nullified the mutual anathemas dating back to 1054. Then, in 1967, the mutual visits of Pope Paul and Patriarch Athenagoras culminated with the common declaration mentioned above, which urged 'a true dialogue of charity' between the Churches, the precious fruit of which would be what Pope John Paul and Patriarch Dimitrios would later call the 'purification of the collective memory of our Churches'.[12] In other words, there was a resolution to start practically loving each other, instead of dwelling on past disputes.

St Paul told the Ephesians to speak the truth in love (Eph 4:15). Ten years or so of setting the necessary context of love made both sides ready, as we might say, to speak the truth. In 1975, on the tenth anniversary of the lifting of the mutual excommunications, Pope Paul made the stunning gesture in the Vatican of kneeling and kissing the feet of the Ecumenical Patriarch's delegate. Colin Davey recalls the reaction of Pierre Duprey, now a bishop and Secretary of the Pontifical Council for Promoting Christian Unity. 'The ceremony might have been no more than a memorial of the past, but it turned into a creative act for the future.' This symbolic action, Duprey continued, 'said more than any speech could have done and demonstrated that the only authority in the Church is that which derives from the humble service of brotherly communion in love and truth'.[13] It was announced on that occasion in 1975 that two commissions, one Catholic and one Orthodox, were to be set up to prepare for the next stage of the theological dialogue.

Early in 1978, a joint coordinating group met in Rome, to sketch out purpose, method and themes. Apparently, a contrast was evident: the Catholic representatives wanted to discuss the differences between the two sides, whereas the Orthodox said that, since we have much more in common than dividing us, we should start with areas of agreement.[14] Thankfully, the latter view prevailed, so as to ensure 'a positive spirit' in the dialogue. It was agreed to start from 'the elements that unite the Orthodox Church and the Roman Catholic Church and move towards the goal which was identified as 'the re-establishment of full communion between the two Churches', a communion which would find its expression 'in the common celebration of the Holy Eucharist'.

In their plan for launching the dialogue, this joint group said that the tradition of the ancient Church considered there to be one great sacrament of Christ on this earth, realised through the power of the Holy Spirit, namely the Church. The Church pre-eminently celebrates herself, expresses and realises herself as the sacrament of Christ in the *communal celebration of the Eucharist*, to which all the other sacraments are linked. The Eucharist was thus put firmly in the spotlight on the basis of the tradition of the early Church, a tradition which is bringing ecumenical convergence in modern ecclesiology as it is reappropriated.[15] This focus on the Eucharist is invaluable as a gauge of the importance of issues. Diversities between the two Churches which are *compatible* with eucharistic communion are not differences to be overcome but a mutual enrichment.[16]

Theological Dialogue

On this basis, when Pope John Paul visited Patriarch Dimitrios in 1979, they both duly launched the Joint Commission for Theological Dialogue between the Roman Catholic Church and the Orthodox Church. Moreover, a definite target in time was set; the Pope urged a hastening 'towards perfect brotherly reconciliation, so that the dawn of the third millennium may find us standing side by side, in full communion, to bear witness together to salvation before the world, the evangelisation of which is waiting for this sign of unity'.[17] In this Decade of Evangelisation or Evangelism, we must renew our awareness of how dramatic a sign of the Good News a united Church would be in a divided world (cf Jn 17:21).

Like Pope Paul and Patriarch Athenagoras before them, Pope John Paul and Patriarch Dimitrios felt at that meeting the pain of not being able to concelebrate.[18] It is good to realise that not only lay people but also Church leaders are familiar with the pain of eucharistic separation.

The Joint Commission met first in 1980 on the Island of Rhodes, resolving to begin with a study of what happens when a local church celebrates the Eucharist. Moving out from this starting point, the delegates were convinced that they would eventually reach all of the main issues that needed to be addressed. The delegates actually number fifty six, determined by there being fourteen Orthodox Churches, each of which contributes a bishop and a theologian, twenty eight Catholic bishops and theologians being then required to achieve a balance. Fifty six is hardly a good working number, hence much of the vital work is done in small subcommissions.

The first topic chosen to be addressed was: 'The Mystery of the Church and of the Eucharist in the Light of the Mystery of the Holy Trinity'.[19] The dialogue has been blessed in many ways, but it has never been blessed with pithy titles! Three subcommissions and then a coordinating committee worked on the topic in 1980-81. A text was finalised at the second plenary meeting of the Joint Commission at Munich in 1982. As already indicated, there have since been two further agreed statements. The second, finally agreed at Bari in 1987, deals with: 'Faith, Sacraments and the Unity of the Church'.[20] The third followed swiftly, just a year later, being accepted in a plenary meeting at Valamo Monastery in Finland. It is entitled: 'The Sacrament of Order in the Sacramental Structure of the Church'.[21]

So, the three common texts deal, first, with the Eucharist, then with the other sacraments and faith, and then with how the Church is structured around bishops by Ordination. The key to the unity of these statements can be found in what the Joint Commission said at its first plenary meeting in 1980.

> 'We hope that restoring full communion among our Churches will contribute to the reconciliation of mankind and to world peace, a reconciliation and peace of which the Church is a sign and a divine instrument in God's will.' [22]

The dialogue, then, looks to the *future*, to reconciliation and peace in God's Kingdom. That future reality is something which the dialogue repeatedly says is brought to bear on the historical present by the *Holy Spirit*, the result here and now being the community of the *Church*, which is the sign and divine instrument of God's purpose of reconciliation and peace.

As we look briefly at the three agreed statements now, let us see this trio of elements recurring constantly: the *future* reality brought to bear on the historical present by the *Holy Spirit* and the effect being the *Church*.

The First Statement

The statement on the Eucharist, in 1982, says: '[t]he ecclesial community is... called to be the outline of a human community renewed' (II,3). The Church, in other words, is a sketch of something yet to come. All of the Church's teaching, government and life are referred to as a prolongation and practical expression of 'that union [between each community and its bishop] expressed in the Eucharist' (II,3). So, the focal preview of future renewal is provided by the eucharistic community. It is in celebrating the Eucharist that '[t]he pilgrim Church... anticipates the judgement of the world and its final transfiguration' (I,4c).How does this happen? How are 'the last times' already present there? Because, as the statement says, '[t]he Eucharist and the Church' are 'the place of the energies of the Holy Spirit' (I,4a). Reiterating the ancient teaching of Ignatius of Antioch and Irenaeus, the statement summarises the Eucharist as 'the foretaste of eternal life, the medicine of immortality, the sign of the Kingdom to come' (I,2).

What is being said is that the Church is most herself when she is celebrating the Eucharist. In other words, what most deserves the name 'Church' is the eucharistic assembly. This is how the Joint Commission understands the fact that, as it says, looking at the New Testament, the Church is a 'local' reality; there are several in a region, each in a given place. Each of these local realities is the result of something breaking in from above.

> '[T]he Church existing in a given place is not formed, in a radical sense, by the persons who come together to establish it. There is a "Jerusalem from on high" which "comes down from God", a communion which is the foundation of the community itself. The Church comes into being by a free gift, that of the new creation' (II,1).

In each local Eucharist, then, by the power of the Holy Spirit, there is an imprint made of the future life of communion in the new Jerusalem. But the archetype for that life of communion, is nothing less than the Trinity. Hence arises the densest sentence of the whole text. 'Taken as a whole,' it says, 'the eucharistic celebration makes present the Trinitarian mystery of the Church' (I,6). In one sentence, there is material for a lifetime's reflection!

There are many celebrations across space and time, but only one imprint is ever made, namely that of the one final Church of God. Bringing out this oneness is clearly essential if the world is to understand the Gospel. In short, apostolic succession is what expresses the oneness through the ages (cf II,4; III,4) and conciliarity or collegiality is what expresses the oneness across the world at a given time in history (cf III,4).

The Second Statement

So, the Eucharist is inseparably linked to the future, the Holy Spirit and the Church. These three elements instantly reappear in what the second statement says about faith and the other sacraments.

Faith, we are told, 'seeks a reorientation towards the realities of the Kingdom which is coming and which, even now, is beginning to transform the realities of this world' (11). There is the future. 'Faith is the result not of a logical elaboration and necessity, but of the influence of the grace of the Holy Spirit' (5). There is the Holy Spirit. Nor, finally, is faith something abstract or vague. 'Given by God, the faith announced by the Church is proclaimed, lived and transmitted in a local, visible church in communion with all the local churches spread over the world, that is, the catholic Church of all times and everywhere' (8). There, then, is the Church, as local eucharistic imprints, woven together through time and space.

All of the sacraments express and strengthen faith and all are essentially bound up with the Eucharist, because that is 'the proclamation of faith *par excellence*' (17). As St Paul told the Corinthians: 'whenever you eat this bread and drink this cup, you *proclaim the Lord's death* until he comes' (1 Cor 11:26).

Now, an important point. Identity of faith is an essential condition for sharing the sacraments, particularly the Eucharist (25). However, East and West have developed differently since their separation, and, in fact, did so for a long time beforehand. What criteria can we formulate together for identifying a true development of faith under the guidance of the Holy Spirit, so that the particular developments on one side can be assessed by the other? The agreed statement gives three criteria for 'legitimate developments' (28). First, they must be in continuity with tradition (29). Secondly, they must be worthy of celebration, in conformity, that is, with the salvation celebrated in the liturgy (30). Thirdly, they must acknowledge our final destiny, which is one of 'deification [*theosis*] through victory over death and in the transfiguration of creation' (31).

It is highly significant that these criteria weight the assessment of agreement in faith in favour of investigating whether we agree on the future destiny to which we are called. This is a liberating principle. The past nine hundred years and more cannot help but divide us, but, if we can agree about our destination, and about how we anticipate it here and now, perhaps we can break the log-jam of grievances and unite.

In support of this principle, we may recall what St Paul tells the Ephesians. 'There is one body and one Spirit', he says, expressing the conviction which underlies all ecumenical effort, and he then goes on to list all the unique factors which unify this Body: 'one Lord, one faith, one baptism, one God and Father of all'. But in the first place, before mentioning any of these factors, he says, 'There is one body and one Spirit, just as you were called to one *hope* when you were called' (Eph 4:4-6). What primarily unites Christians in one Body is the single *hope* which we have, as we look *forward*.

The New Testament gives ample evidence of hope being a prime distinguishing characteristic of the early Christians. St Paul tells the Thessalonians that they are known throughout the whole region as people who gave up idols in order to serve the true God and who are now *waiting* for God's Son from heaven (cf 1 Thess 1:9-10). At Mass, the community is still said to be *waiting* 'in joyful hope for the coming of our Saviour, Jesus Christ'. If we can rekindle in our day that forward-looking hope, derived first and foremost from the Eucharist, perhaps we can restore the unity which springs from it.

The Third Statement

Turning now to the third agreed statement, on Ordination and ministry in the Church, we find the discussion set in the context of the ministry which, as we acknowledged earlier, the Church has as a whole to the world. How does the Church serve the world? By giving it hope in the future. The text says: 'all ministries are intended to serve the world so as to lead it to its true goal, the Kingdom of God' (12). The primary means by which the Church renders this service is by making that goal present for the world when she gathers for the Eucharist. The Eucharist, we are told, 'makes already present the world to come' (36). The eucharistic assembly 'is an anticipation of the final community with Christ' (14).

Again, this time regarding the topic of ministry, we are immediately linking it to the future and to the Church. Given that the primary ministry exercised by the Church is to reveal the future in the Eucharist, it follows that the primary ministry *in* the Church is that of *presiding* at the Eucharist. First and foremost, this is the task of the *bishop*. 'It is in presiding over the eucharistic assembly that the role of the bishop finds its accomplishment' (41). It is out of this eucharistic role that all of the bishop's teaching and government flow (38, 39). His identity as 'the icon of Christ' (33) derives from this *eucharistic* role, where, indeed, he stands in the midst of his local church as Christ in the midst of the final gathering of all the ages in the heavenly Jerusalem (cf Heb 12:22-24 and Rev 14:1). That is the important visual parallel which is implicit in these statements. Completing the trio of elements, we note that the one who enables this eschatological presence is none other than the Holy Spirit, constituting here, as ever, in the words of the Joint Commission, 'the earnest of the perfect realisation of God's design for the world' (3, cf 10).

The statement recalls the most ancient practice of the Church that a new bishop is ordained by at least two or three other bishops (27). This practice, we may note, is not a safeguard for validity, lest one of them says the wrong words or has evil intent. No, it is simply that two or three are the minimum requirements for a community. It was surely for this reason that the Lord himself said that where two or three were gathered in his name, he would be there in their midst (Mt 18:20). The manner of episcopal Ordination clearly expresses that the Lord's presence in a local church, via its bishop, is a presence enjoyed in the communion of local churches and in the fraternity of their bishops.

Thereafter, bishops express the communion of their churches by coming together in councils (54). But we may rightly comment that councils, of their nature, are sporadic; they convene and disperse. Is there not a permanent structural manifestation of fraternity that the Lord intended for his Church? Around perhaps a central guardian of unity? This is a crucial question.

The statement does note that, in the ancient Church which is our common heritage, in each region there was a recognised *first* bishop, without whose agreement the others could not act and who equally required the agreement of the others for his own actions (53). There was, then, a stable structure of communion in each *region*. But to what extent was there a universal primacy exercised by Rome? The Joint Commission honestly admitted that this was a question 'which constitutes a serious divergence between us and which will be discussed in the future' (55).

Difficulties

That, in short, is where we now stand. A fourth agreed statement is prepared, entitled: 'Conciliarity and Authority in the Church'. It gives further consideration to the matters treated in the third statement and would have been finalised at the plenary meeting in 1990 in Freising, had it not been for the sudden re-emergence of the dispute over Uniate Churches. The new spirit of openness in Eastern Europe has brought recognition of formerly repressed Eastern communities in union with Rome. But old wounds have also opened up and the dialogue is effectively stalled until Catholics and Orthodox heal them with loving respect for one another. This problem, said a joint declaration, now has 'priority over all other subjects to be discussed in the dialogue'.[23]

In June, 1991, a draft statement on this intermediate issue was completed, significantly entitled: 'Uniatism, Former Method of Union, and the Present Search for Full Communion'. Following the death of Dimitrios I and the election of his successor as Ecumenical Patriarch, Bartolomeos I, late in 1991, this text was due for discussion at the plenary meeting which was scheduled for June, 1992, but which now will take place in 1993.

Has the dialogue, otherwise, been trouble-free? No, it would be wrong to give that impression. The language of the statements has provoked some reaction. One Greek professor, himself actually a member of the original Joint Commission, objected that the language of the statement on the Eucharist was 'existential', by which he meant, he said, 'incomprehensible and... far from traditional doctrinal definitions'. The text was 'neutral and impersonal', he complained, 'lacking the character of either the Orthodox or Roman Catholic tradition'. We should start, he urged, from our distinct positions and then try to put them together.[24]

Then there can be misunderstandings and clashes of temperament, as when the delegations from Greece and Jerusalem failed to attend the plenary meeting in 1986 because they considered that a Vatican exhibition of icons from Macedonia implied Catholic recognition of the Macedonian Orthodox Church, which other Orthodox Churches regard as schismatic. The

Cypriot and Serbian delegations did come... but then walked out.[25]

There can be opposition by members of one Church to the status of the other Church. This is more often found on the Orthodox side. An admittedly extreme example would be the complaint that went from Mount Athos to Patriarch Dimitrios on his return from that momentous visit to the Pope in 1987, in which he had participated in the Liturgy of the Word at Mass in St Peter's. According to the monks: 'the sacraments of the Roman Church are devoid of grace... this participation in heretical worship was unacceptable'.[26]

Finally, there is an awkward problem which must honestly be located mainly on the Catholic side. There are those who would question the whole assumption of the dialogue that the insights of the early Church can indeed teach us and renew us in our ecclesial life today; those who would even say that the early Church, far from being exemplary, was actually mistaken in key areas. Someone of that opinion is not going to have much time for this dialogue!

Conclusion

We have seen that the practical focus of Catholic-Orthodox dialogue so far has been the Eucharist, intimately bound up with the future, the Holy Spirit and the Church community. This trio of elements underpins all of the agreed statements. Though only a small number of people are directly involved in official Catholic-Orthodox dialogue, a powerful way in which members of both Churches can *all* participate is by allowing their understanding of the role of these three elements in the Eucharist to develop.

To pray, reflect and discuss with these perhaps new perspectives is truly to sow the seeds of unity, or, better, is truly to prepare the ground to receive in good soil the seeds of unity which only the Lord can sow. He does so principally in the Eucharist, as we recognise just before Communion in every Mass when we recall his words: 'I leave you peace; my own peace I give you' (cf Jn 14:27). Catholic-Orthodox unity will be accomplished in the very act of Catholics and Orthodox being *together* to receive this gift once again in the Eucharist; from then on, being one.

What has brought a renewed appreciation of the trio of elements we have highlighted? Where have these theological ideas come from? The answer surely lies in the Fathers of the Church. Their writings are widely accessible to us now as they have never been to previous generations of Christians. Scholarship and technology have set them readily before us in recent decades. For example, a foundational text by Hippolytus, his *Apostolic Tradition* from the early third century, was thought for hundreds of years to have been lost until a researcher in 1910 located and identified it. Now it is on many shelves.

One leading Orthodox theologian, John Zizioulas, who is now Metropolitan of Pergamon, has acknowledged that 'the return to the ancient patristic sources, which has characterised Western theology in our century, is largely responsible for the Orthodox theological renaissance'.[27] He singles out the contribution of one Catholic scholar in particular, namely, Henri de Lubac, who died in 1991, at the age of 95. Zizioulas, in fact, was a founding member of the Catholic-Orthodox international dialogue and is one of the principal drafters of the three statements we have examined.[28]

So many of the early Fathers predate our divisions.

Their perspectives can bring us together. What they often do, in fact, is to return us to the profound simplicity of the New Testament, as we may finally note. After all, if we look closely, we will find that trio of elements in the writings of St John. It is, very significantly, in the context of the Last Supper in John's Gospel that Jesus says: 'When the Spirit of truth comes... he will tell you of the things to come' (Jn 16:13). The Spirit reveals the things to come in the setting of the Eucharist.

Then, in the Book of Revelation, John tells us of the vision he had when the Spirit caught him up and showed him the things to come, on the Lord's Day, that is, the day when he surely celebrated the Eucharist. He saw a great gathering, the Lamb surrounded by the elders and the multitudes, on Mount Zion, in the heavenly Jerusalem (e.g. Rev 4:2-4; 7:9; 14:1; cf the visual parallel highlighted above). The author of the Letter to the Hebrews tells us of the same vision, giving us sufficient clues to locate it likewise in the context of the Eucharist. Moreover, in what is perhaps the purest use of this term in the New Testament, he calls this gathering '[the] Church' ('*ekklesía*'; Heb 12:22-24). So, already in the New Testament, we find the future, the Spirit and the Church, all bound up with the Eucharist.

John tells us that he saw his vision on the island of Patmos, where he had been exiled for preaching God's word and witnessing to Jesus (Rev 1:9). The first plenary meeting of the Catholic-Orthodox dialogue took place on the island of Rhodes. However, before moving on to Rhodes, the delegates made a pilgrimage, which may now be seen as full of significance. Where did they go? To the island of Patmos.

May St John and the holy Mother he was given at

the foot of the Cross continue to intercede for this dialogue, that it may surmount its recent difficulties and reach its goal, carried forward by the blessed spirit in which it began.

NOTES

1. E. J. Stormon (ed. and trans.), *Towards the Healing of Schism. The Sees of Rome and Constantinople. Public statements and correspondence between the Holy See and the Ecumenical Patriarchate, 1958-1984* (Paulist Press, New York/Mahwah, 1987), pp. 144-145. This exhaustive book is an invaluable resource.
2. *Ibid.*, p.155.
3. Cf Eleuterio Fortino, 'The Catholic-Orthodox dialogue', *One in Christ*, 18(1982), p. 194.
4. Stormon, *Towards the Healing of Schism*, p. 155.
5. *Ibid.*, p. 169.
6. *Ibid.*, p. 172.
7. Fortino, 'The Catholic-Orthodox dialogue', p. 194.
8. Secretariat (now Pontifical Council) for Promoting Christian Unity (hereafter PCPCU), *Information Service*, n. 66, 1988(I), p. 25.
9. J. Ratzinger, *Das neue Volk Gottes* (Patmos Verlag, Düsseldorf, 1969), part 2, chapter 4
10. The text may be found in another important collection of documents: Constantin G. Patelos (ed.), *The Orthodox Church in the Ecumenical Movement* (World Council of Churches, Geneva, 1978), pp. 40-43.
11. Fortino, 'The Catholic-Orthodox dialogue', p. 195.
12. *Ibid.*, p. 198.
13. Colin Davey, 'Orthodox-Roman Catholic Dialogue', *One in Christ* 20(1984), p.348. This article and Colin Davey's two further articles in *One in Christ*, 1990/1991, give much valuable information on the historical course of the dialogue.
14. *Ibid.*, p. 349. Also for the further quotations in this paragraph.
15. Cf Paul McPartlan, 'Eucharistic Ecclesiology', *One in Christ*, 22(1986), pp. 314-331.
16. Cf Fortino, 'The Catholic-Orthodox dialogue', p. 199.
17. This setting of the year 2000 as a target was recalled by Cardinal Willebrands in Istanbul on the tenth anniversary of Pope John Paul's visit: cf PCPCU, *Information Service*, n. 73, 1990(II), p. 30.
18. Cf Davey, 'Orthodox-Roman Catholic Dialogue', p. 351. After his return to Rome, the Pope said that he had gone 'in order to show before God and before the whole people of God my impatience for unity'. 'We felt painfully how regrettable it was that we could not concelebrate. Everything must be done to hasten the day of this concelebration.'

19. See above, pp. 37-52. Numbers in parentheses will give the location of quotations from this and the other texts.
20. See above, pp. 53-69.
21. See above, pp. 71-86.
22. Fortino, 'The Catholic-Orthodox dialogue', p. 203.
23. PCPCU, *Information Service*, n.73, 1990(II), p. 52.
24. Cf Davey, 'Orthodox-Roman Catholic Dialogue', pp. 360- 361.
25. Davey, '"Clearing a path through a minefield": Orthodox-Roman Catholic Dialogue, 1983-1990', *One in Christ,* 26(1990), p. 289.
26. *Ibid.*, p. 302.
27. J. Zizioulas, 'Ortodossía', in *Enciclopedia del Novecento*, vol. 5 (Istituto della Enciclopedia Italiana, Roma, 1980), p. 6.
28. A good way to explore the theological perspectives of the agreed statements is to read, e.g., Zizioulas' book, *Being as Communion* (Darton, Longman & Todd, London, 1986), which strongly features the trio of elements we have identified and focuses upon the Eucharist. I have analysed and compared the theology of de Lubac and Zizioulas in my book: *The Eucharist Makes the Church. Henri de Lubac and John Zizioulas in dialogue* (T. & T. Clark, Edinburgh, 1992).

Praying with Icons
Bishop Kallistos of Diokleia*

There's glory for you!
Humpty Dumpty (Lewis Carroll, *Through the Looking Glass)*

A Liturgical Art

Our best approach to any Christian community not our
own – our best approach, equally, to any non-Christian
faith – is to ask ourselves the question: How do its
members pray? What form does their worship take,
what is their sense of the sacred or the numinous? In
what manner do they stand before God? For Western
Christians, then, seeking to understand the Orthodox
tradition, the most helpful way of opening a window is
to be present, not once but many times, at the celebration of the Divine Liturgy. Anyone who does that
cannot but notice the role played by the icon in Orthodox prayer. When an Orthodox Christian stands before
God, he or she stands before the holy icons. In the
words of the most influential icon painter of the twen-
tieth-century Russian emigration, Leonid Ouspensky
(1902-1987), 'It is absolutely impossible to imagine
the smallest liturgical rite in the Orthodox Church
without icons. The liturgical and sacramental life of
the Church is inseparable from the image.'[1]

In my own first experience of Orthodox worship,
which I can recall most vividly, the icons played a
decisive part. One Saturday afternoon nearly forty

* See pp.169-170 for details of Contributors.

years ago, while still a schoolboy, on an impulse I went inside the Russian church in London – then at St Philip's, Buckingham Palace Road (soon afterwards destroyed, to make way for extensions to Victoria Coach Station) – and I found the Vigil service in progress. Everything was in Slavonic, and so with my conscious brain I understood not a single word. But I was struck at once by two things, by an absence and by a presence. The few worshippers were standing close to the walls, and so my initial impression, as I entered the dark cavernous interior, was of a vast expanse of polished floor. I was surprised by the emptiness, by the absence of pews or rows of chairs. This first feeling, however, was swiftly replaced by another far more profound and powerful. I became aware of a presence – the presence of icons on the walls and on the icon-screen; and not only of that, but of the presence, mediated through these icons, of countless unseen worshippers. I felt that the church was not empty but full.

Without at that moment formulating my thoughts in words, intuitively I understood that this small congregation was part of a much greater whole. We, the visible worshippers, were being taken up into an action far greater than ourselves, into an all-embracing drama that united earth and heaven through the presence of the holy icons. The liturgical space of the church was 'heaven on earth', to use a phrase much loved by Orthodox Christians. When, several years afterwards, I first attended the Lenten Presanctified Liturgy and heard the hymn sung by the choir at the Great Entrance, 'Now the powers of heaven worship with us invisibly', my heart burnt within me; for such exactly had been my own experience on that Saturday afternoon. I realize now that many of the icons which I

142

saw in St Philip's were painted in a debased Italianate idiom, not in the true Byzantine style, but that did not worry me at the time. What mattered then, and what matters to me still, is the sense of presence which the icons conveyed.

If my first encounter with the icon occurred during an act of prayer, that was entirely as it should be. Some years ago I read an article in the colour supplement of The Observer, containing interviews with people who owned icons. (Yet, do we ever 'own' an icon? Surely it is with icons as with cats: they do not belong to us but we belong to them.) Most of those included in the article strove to express, somewhat inarticulately, the distinctive effect produced by the icons hanging on their walls: 'They're very private and personal... I couldn't eat in front of them.' (Incidentally a Greek or Russian Christian would find nothing odd about eating in front of an icon.) Only one person came to the heart of the matter, the late Count Alexis Bobrinskoy. Asked what part his icons played in his life, he answered briefly, 'I pray before them'. In that simple reply he summed up the one essential point about the icon. *We pray with our icons.* As the Orthodox writer Philip Sherrard affirms, 'An icon divorced from a place and act of worship is a contradiction in terms.'[2] Prayer and the icon are inseparably united. The icon is a form of prayer. The art of the icon is a liturgical art.

The bond between iconography and prayer is clearly evident from the way in which an icon is made. Prayer is present at every stage in the preparation. 'Only saints can paint icons', says Fr Paul Florensky (1882-?1943), the Russian theologian-mathematician who died as a confessor for the faith under Stalin.[3] Icon-painting presupposes not only technical skill but purity of heart. It is a vocation from the Holy Spirit, to be approached with awe and humility. 'Do not just carry out this work haphazardly, but with the fear of God and with the veneration due to a sacred task', states the eighteenth-century Greek *Painter's Manual* compiled by Dionysius of Fourna. '... This is a heavenly task given by God.'[4] According to the Stoglav Council held at Moscow in 1551, 'The painter should be humble and meek, full of reverence, not given to idle talk and jesting. He should not be quarrelsome or envious, not a drunkard or a murderer. Above all, with the utmost care he will preserve spiritual and bodily purity... He will make frequent visits to his spiritual father for confession, revealing everything to him, continuing in fasting and prayer according to his guidance, and avoiding all shamelessness and disorder.' Particularly significant is the insistence here upon spiritual direction, upon the need for close personal contact with an elder or *starets*. The Council adds that, before embarking on his work, the future iconographer is to be brought before the bishop to be blessed.[5] Today it is more usual for the blessing to be conferred by the spiritual father. Whatever the practice, it is clear that the iconographer is a person set apart by the authority of the Church. Icon-painting is not merely a private pursuit, depending on an individual choice, but it is an ecclesial ministry validated by God's blessing.

There is in fact a special liturgical office for the commissioning of an iconographer. In the rite contained in the *Painter's Manual* by Dionysius of Fourna, the main prayer recalls the tradition that the first icon-painter was St Luke the Evangelist, who portrayed the Mother of God. The officiant continues: 'Illumine and bring wisdom to the soul and heart and mind of your servant and direct these his [her] hands... to your glory and to the splendour and beautifying of your holy

Church.'⁶ Also included in the service is the *troparion* or office hymn for the feast of the Transfiguration (6 August). Just as the Transfiguration of Christ on Mount Tabor was a revelation of divine glory and beauty, so each icon makes manifest God's glory in the world. Often the first icon that the newly-blessed apprentice is made to paint is the Transfiguration, not that this is by any means the easiest theme to depict, but because every icon is an extension of the mystery of the Transfiguration.

As a preparation, then, for this 'heavenly task' given by God, the iconographer requires not merely an outer training in pictorial techniques but also, and much more fundamentally, an inner formation through *ascesis* and prayer. While it is important that the person who paints an icon should be artistically gifted, it is yet more important that he or she should be a committed member of the Church – one who prays and fasts, and who regularly receives the sacraments of Confession and Holy Communion, thereby participating to the full in the total context of belief and devotion to which the icon itself belongs. Moreover, during the actual painting of an icon, the iconographer will seek to be continually immersed in prayer. While working he will no more think of smoking or of listening to a comedy show on the radio than he would think of smoking or listening to the radio during his morning prayers.⁷ In the case of the great icon-painters, the creative beauty of the icon filled their imagination not only during their hours of work but in their leisure time as well. It is recounted of St Andrew Rublëv (c.1370-c.1430) that on Easter Sunday he and his fellow painters 'sat before the divine and revered icons and ceaselessly gazed at them, filled with godlike joy and light; and this they did, not only on that day, but also on the other days when they did not paint'.[8] For them, iconography was not a temporary occupation but a total way of life.

Painted in this manner with prayer and contemplative wonder, the icon once completed is then introduced into the liturgical life of the Church. This may be done in various ways. In earlier times it seems that no specific prayers of blessing were said over it, and for this very reason the eighth-century iconoclasts – the 'icon-smashers', who tried to secure the removal and destruction of all icons within the Byzantine Empire – maintained that the icon should not be revered as holy. In response to this, the Seventh Ecumenical Council (Nicaea II, A.D.787), which affirmed in its definitive form the Orthodox faith concerning the holy icons, stated that an icon is sanctified through the act of inscribing the name of God or of a saint upon it; but the Council mentioned no special prayers or other ceremony of consecration.[9] Even today in the Greek practice it is often considered sufficient to leave an icon in the sanctuary for forty days, without saying any particular blessing over it. The Greek editions, however, of the *Great Euchologion* or 'Book of Prayers' do in fact include a rite for the blessing of an icon: it is to be anointed with Holy Chrism (though this is something that I have never seen actually done) and a prayer is said over it. The service books used in the Russian Church provide several alternative prayers of blessing, at the end of which the icon is sprinkled with holy water and censed.[10] Sometimes an icon is blessed at the conclusion of the Divine Liturgy simply by being touched with the chalice that contains the Body and Blood of Christ.

Whatever the exact form of the blessing and dedication, its basic significance is the same: the icon is thereby incorporated outwardly and visibly into the Church's worship. It becomes a *holy* icon, a sacramental sign, part of our liturgical and personal prayer, and from this point onwards it receives marks of reverence during church services and at other times. Incense is offered to it, and lamps and candles are lit before it. Bows and prostrations are made in front of it, it is kissed and carried in procession. Normally the first thing that an Orthodox will do on entering church is to venerate the icons and light candles in their honour. This is one of the most important ways in which young children come to feel involved in the liturgical *praxis* of the worshipping community. The same signs of respect are shown to the icons which each Orthodox keeps at home. It is customary to have at least one icon in every room; besides this, traditionally there is a special icon corner or shelf, either in the living room or in the main bedroom, before which family prayers may be said. At home, as in church, icons are honoured with lamps and lighted candles, and incense is offered before them. This is seen more particularly as the task of the mother in the household; by virtue of the royal priesthood conferred on her at Baptism, she presides over the domestic liturgy.

Alike in our corporate worship and in our personal prayers, the icons are our constant companions. They are never out of our sight for long, and virtually everything that we do is carried out in their presence. They sanctify each action, bridging the gap between the secular and the sacred, and introducing the dimension of the transcendent into all aspects of our daily existence.

An Opened Door

Everything that has been said so far about the icon as living prayer shows how altogether inadequate it is to describe icons merely as religious pictures. They are much more than that. 'The icon is a door', states the life of St Stephen the Younger (d. c. 764), who underwent martyrdom in defence of the holy icons.[11] It is a means of entry, a place of meeting.

Entry into what? Meeting with whom? St John of Damascus (c.675-c. 749) supplies the answer: 'When we venerate an icon, we do not offer veneration to matter, but through the icon we venerate the person depicted on it. For, as St Basil says, "The honour given to the icon passes to the prototype".'[12] Note here the careful use of the preposition *through*, emphasizing that the icon is not an end in itself but a channel of communication. It fulfils a mediatorial function: its role is mystagogic, it initiates us. *Through* the icon we pass within the dimensions of sacred space and sacred time, attaining the point of intersection between the earthly and the heavenly, between the temporal and the eternal. *Through* the icon we are brought directly face to face with the one whom it portrays, whether this is Christ the Saviour, his Mother, an angel or a saint. The icon, that is to say, does not simply 'represent' these persons in an artistic manner but it 're-presents' them, it *makes them present.* As Paul Evdokimov (1901-1970) rightly observes, the theology of the icon is a 'theology of presence'.[13] The icon is thus our means of entry into the communion of saints, our place of meeting with the glorified Church in heaven.

Once the icon is understood in this way as an opened door, as a means of entry and a presence, the icon-screen or iconostasis that dominates the interior of most Orthodox churches acquires a significance diametrically opposite to that which a non-Orthodox visitor might imagine it to possess. So far from hiding the

148

action of the Liturgy from the congregation and cutting them off from the sanctuary, its true purpose is to make manifest and unite. It shows us eternity in a concrete, irrefutable form. 'The iconostasis conceals nothing from the faithful', says Fr Paul Florensky. 'It bears witness to the mystery; it discloses to everyone, to the lame and the halt, the entrance to the other world.'[14] According to St Symeon of Thessalonica (d. 1429), the horizontal beam of the iconostasis signifies the union through love between earth and heaven; the main icons of Christ and his Mother that appear on either side of the Holy Doors are an indication that he and she are dwelling simultaneously on high in the heavenly places and also here below with us *at this very moment.*[15] Through the mediation of the iconostasis, we enter into direct communion with the 'great cloud of witnesses' (Heb 12:1) in the Church triumphant. The screen is not a barrier but a meeting-point.

As a place of meeting and a presence, the icon acts as a means of grace, conveying strength, healing and holiness. This is clearly stated by the Seventh Ecumenical Council: 'When we embrace an icon and offer to it the veneration of honour, we share in sanctification.'[16] 'We should believe', says St Theodore the Studite (759-826), 'that divine grace is present in the icon of Christ, and imparts sanctification to those who approach it with faith.'[17] On the Sunday of Orthodoxy – the First Sunday in Lent, celebrating the final restoration of the icons at Constantinople in 842-843 – the liturgical texts proclaim: 'From your icon, O Lord, we receive the grace of healing... the eyes of the beholders are sanctified by the holy icons.'[18] Particular icons that have acted as a focus for prayer and for bodily or inner healing are honoured in the Orthodox Church as 'wonder-working' or miraculous; but in principle every icon without exception is miraculous, an efficacious sacramental sign.

When we speak in such terms about God's presence and grace within the icon, there is an obvious need to guard against superstitious exaggeration; and in practice the Christian East has often failed to do this with sufficient vigilance. The Seventh Ecumenical Council, however, was most careful to draw a sharply-marked distinction between *latreia* or worship in the strict sense, which may rightly be ascribed to God the Trinity alone, and veneration or *schetike time*, 'relative' or 'relational honour', which is given to icons. To quote the dogmatic decree of the Council, 'To these icons one may render the veneration of honour (*time*), but not the true worship (*latreia*) of our faith, which is due only to the divine nature.'[19] We honour icons, but we do not worship them; we pray before them, but we do not pray to them. The icon is a sacramental symbol, not an idol.

In this connection the Council insisted upon a clear differentiation of levels between the icon and the consecrated elements at the Eucharist. The iconoclasts had argued, at the Council of Hieria (754), that the only possible icon of the Saviour is the consecrated Bread and Wine at the Liturgy. To this the Ecumenical Council of 787 replied that the consecrated elements are not merely an icon of our Lord, but they are in full actuality the 'proper Body and Blood of Christ',[20] and as such they receive worship (*latreia*). But an icon of Christ, although mediating his presence and communicating his grace, remains wood and paint, and so it is not worshipped. Christ is truly present alike in the eucharistic elements and in an icon, but the nature of his presence is by no means the same in these two cases.

Unfortunately, due in part to a defective Latin translation of the acts of the Seventh Council, this crucial distinction between *latreia* and *time* was at first misunderstood in the West. Although from the start the Papacy accepted the decrees of Nicaea II, to the north of the Alps they were repudiated by Charlemagne and the Frankish theologians of his *entourage*, who falsely accused the Greeks of adoring icons with the worship due only to the Holy Trinity. Influenced by this misinterpretation, the Councils of Frankfurt (794) and Paris (825) adopted a semi-iconoclast position, decreeing that icons may be displayed in church for decorative or didactic purposes, but should not be venerated with liturgical honour. Not until the eleventh century was the Seventh Council generally accepted in the West as Ecumenical; indeed, it may be doubted whether Latin Christendom has ever fully assimilated the theology of the icon, as this is understood in the Orthodox tradition.

Pace Charlemagne, Orthodox Christians have always known perfectly well that they are not worshipping wood and paint. I recall hearing once from the abbess of the Russian Orthodox convent in North London about a visit from some Protestant friends. Seeing the Orthodox faithful venerating the icons in the chapel, they began to murmur about idolatry. 'Tell me', asked the abbess, 'do you honour the Bible?' 'Of course we do', they replied. 'What!' she exclaimed. 'Do you worship ink and paper?' Just as an Evangelical Christian in the West worships not ink and paper but the living Word who speaks to us through ink and paper, so an Orthodox Christian worships not wood and paint but the living Saviour whom we encounter *through* the wood and paint of the icon.

Occasionally it is claimed that, because an icon is

151

two-dimensional, not solid like a Western statue, the danger of idolatry is reduced. This line of argument rests on a misunderstanding. The point at issue in the Byzantine iconoclast controversy of the eighth and ninth centuries was the legitimacy or otherwise of making *any* representational image of the human figure in religious art. Neither side seems to have attached doctrinal significance to the distinction between images in two dimensions and those in three. The Seventh Ecumenical Council does not in fact differentiate between flat pictures and solid statues; and nowhere does it lay down any restrictions concerning the material or medium to be employed in the making of icons. An icon does not have to be a panel painting on wood; it may take the form of a mosaic or fresco, a miniature in a manuscript, an embroidery, or a likeness executed in metal or enamel. It can also be a reproduction printed on paper or on cloth; although certain rigorists deny that something mass-produced in this way can be a true icon, their opinion is sufficiently refuted by the Orthodox experience in America, where several of the miracle-working 'weeping' icons, which I myself have seen, are printed paper reproductions. The Celtic 'high crosses' in Ireland and Northumbria can justly be regarded as icons; and so by the same token can a statue.

Free-standing, three-dimensional figures are certainly infrequent in the religious art of the Christian East, but they are not altogether unknown. There is a well-known story about St Theodora, the wife of the iconoclast emperor Theophilus (829-842), which suggests that statues may well have been in use among Byzantine Christians at this time. The court fool found her praying before the icons and told the emperor. When he indignantly upbraided her, she replied that she had simply been playing with her 'dolls' (*ninia*). This makes better sense if what she had been venerating was a statuette, not a flat picture.[21] Visitors to the Byzantine section of the Victoria and Albert Museum in London will be familiar with the beautiful twelfth-century statuette of the Mother of God *Hodegetria* ('She who shows the way').[22] Wooden statues are to be found in Northern Russia during the medieval period, although Western influence may possibly account for this. Relatively rare though they may be, such examples are sufficient to disprove the view that Orthodoxy forbids all statues on principle.

Art as Tradition and Contemplation

'If you are a theologian,' states an often-quoted Orthodox maxim, 'you will pray in truth; and if you pray truly, you are a theologian.'[23] Dogmas are nothing else than the crystallization of that which the saints have experienced in prayer, while prayer in its turn is the dogmas of the faith affirmed existentially. Since there is this integral link between prayer and theology, the art of the icon, as a liturgical art – as part of an act of worship – is also an essentially *theological* art. It is 'theology in colour', to use the title of Prince Eugene Trubetskoi's book. The iconographer therefore expresses not merely his private aesthetic emotions but the mind and vision of the Church. His art is not subjective but catholic. It bears witness to Holy Tradition.

The significance of the icon as one of the expressions of ecclesial tradition is a master-theme throughout the dogmatic decree of the Seventh Ecumenical Council. 'We preserve all the traditions of the Church', the Fathers of Nicaea state, 'which for our sake have been decreed in written or unwritten form, without introducing any innovation. One of these traditions is the making of iconographic representations.' Developing the point, the decree goes on to insist upon the close parallelism between the icon and the Book of the Gospels. The pictorial testimony of the icon, the Council maintains, is in total harmony with the verbal narrative of the Gospels; both signify the same thing and both are honoured liturgically with 'the same kind of veneration'.[24] The Gospel is an icon in words, an icon is the Gospel in line and colour. The Gospel is the mystery proclaimed, while an icon is the mystery depicted. In the words of St John of Damascus, 'What speech is to hearing, the icon is to sight.'[25] *Eikon* and *logos* complement each other.

This complementarity is expounded with particular clarity by the Council of Constantinople held in 869-870.

'We declare that the holy icon of our Lord Jesus Christ is to be venerated with the same honour as is given to the Book of the Holy Gospels. Just as we all attain salvation through the letters written in the Book of the Gospels, so all of us alike, whether learned or unlearned, benefit from iconography in colour. What the written word proclaims through syllables, iconography proclaims and renders present to us through colours.'[26]

It is noteworthy that the term 'iconography' means literally not the painting but the *writing* of icons. A recent work on the icon has been aptly entitled *Writing in Gold.*[27]

As an expression of Tradition, parallel to the Gospel, the icon is one of the ways in which the Church teaches the faith. Its didactic value is frequently mentioned by Orthodox writers. 'Icons are opened books, placed in the churches to remind us of God', says St Leontios of Cyprus (7th century).[28] In the words of John of Jerusalem, one of the delegates at Nicaea II: 'If a pagan comes to you and says, "Show me your faith, that I too may believe", what will you show him? Will you not lead him up from visible things to that which is invisible?... And let me tell you how... Take him into the church; show him how it is decorated; set him in front of the holy icons.'[29] In Kievan Russia, St Andrew, prince of Bogoliubov (d.1174), did exactly this with the foreigners who visited him. 'Take them into the church', he said to his servants, 'and put them in the gallery, that they may see true Christianity and accept Baptism.'[30]

Since the icon is in this way part of Tradition, an expression of the Church's doctrinal teaching, it is not to be regarded simply as a work of art, any more than the Bible is to be regarded simply as a work of literature. What matters is not primarily the style of an icon or its artistic quality but its accuracy as a witness to the revealed truth. In the eloquent words of Fr Paul Florensky, 'The Church's idea of art was, is and shall be one alone – *realism*. This means that the Church, which is *the pillar and ground of truth*, insists upon one thing only, and that is TRUTH.'[31] It is vital to keep in mind the literal connotation of the term *eikon*: it signifies 'reflection'. An icon is to be held in honour, not for its aesthetic character as a self-contained 'art object', but for its authenticity as a reflection of eternal truth. Its beauty, however great, has no meaning or value apart from its truth.

Transmitting as he does the orthodox and catholic

tradition of the Church, the painter of an icon is not free to invent and innovate as the fancy takes him. An essential element in his spiritual formation is obedience, *kenosis*. He is a witness and is therefore called to become transparent, so that the light of God's revelation can shine through his handiwork. He has to allow the Holy Spirit to guide his fingers. Artistic creativity is by no means excluded – the true iconographer is not a slavish copyist, nor is iconography on a level with the production of imitation antique furniture – but his creativity is exercised according to certain norms inherited from Holy Tradition. In the words of the Seventh Ecumenical Council, 'The making of icons does not depend upon the invention of painters, but is an accepted institution and tradition of the Catholic Church... The conception and tradition of the icons derive from the Fathers, not from the painter. The painter's domain is limited to his art, while the content and arrangement of the icons is from the Holy Fathers.'[32] The true iconographers, as Fr Paul Florensky points out, are the Holy Fathers themselves.[33]

This means that the art of the icon is not only a liturgical and theological art but above all a contemplative art. The point is finely expressed by Philip Sherrard: 'Whereas in non-iconographic art the picture is generally conceived as expressing the artist's own response to or observation of his subject, it is more true in the case of an icon to think of the sacred subject itself projecting or reflecting itself on to the material of the icon... The artist, that is, has to become one with that which he is to represent. In other words, there is here no distinction between art and contemplation.'[34]

When Dr Sherrard speaks in this way about the sacred subject 'projecting itself' on to the material of the icon, among other things he has in view the well-known story of Abgar, King of Edessa, and the Mandilion. Prevented from meeting Christ in person, Abgar sent a painter to make a portrait of our Lord. This the artist was unable to do because of the dazzling light which shone from the Saviour; so Christ pressed a cloth on his face, and when this was removed his likeness was found to be miraculously imprinted upon it.[35] This cloth, the Mandilion which Christ sent to Abgar – the icon 'not made with hands' (*acheiropoietos*), as it is termed – is regarded in Orthodoxy as *the* original icon of Christ, the source of all other icons. Before we dismiss the story of Abgar as a 'legend' let us reflect on the all-important truth that it embodies: a genuine icon is not invented but revealed.

The Human Face of God

In what particular ways does the icon as 'theology in colour' bear witness to the Tradition of the Church? There are, above all, three aspects of the Christian revelation that it safeguards and proclaims: it expresses the truth about Christ, about the world and about our human personhood.

1. The icon and the Incarnation

The icon protects the central affirmation of the Fourth Gospel, 'The Word became flesh' (Jn 1:14). Salvation for the Christian believer is not an abstract theory but a particular Person, the second member of the Trinity, who lived out on earth a fully human existence in a concrete and palpable form, assuming both a human soul and a physical body. 'That which was from the beginning,' writes the apostle, 'which we have heard, which we have seen with our own eyes, which we have looked at and touched with our hands...that is what we declare to you' (1Jn 1:1-3). *Heard, seen, touched*: salvation is specific, visible, tangible. It is exactly this specific, visible, tangible character of salvation that the icon of Christ guarantees and makes manifest.

God did not simply appear on earth in some shadowy and insubstantial form, but he made his own a true human soul and likewise a true human body formed of the same physical elements as our bodies are. Because Christ has assumed in this way authentic and integral humanity, it is possible to make a pictorial representation of him as God incarnate. Indeed, it is not only *possible* to do this, but also *necessary*; for to refuse to make an icon of Christ is to imply that his human nature is somehow unreal. As the Seventh Ecumenical Council insists, the icon confirms that 'the Incarnation of God the Word is real and not illusory'.[36] Behind iconoclasm the Fathers of Nicaea II saw the spectre of docetism.

Critics of the holy icons, whether in ancient or in modern times, regularly appeal to the second of the Ten Commandments (Ex 20:4), which forbids any visual representation of God. What such an argument overlooks is precisely the connection between the icon and the Incarnation. The prohibition of images, St John of Damascus observes, was entirely reasonable in the period of the Old Testament, before Christ's Incarnation had taken place. But everything has now been altered by the event of Nazareth and Bethlehem:

'If we attempted to make an icon of the invisible God, that would be sinful indeed... It is impossible to make an icon of God the incorporeal, the invisible, the non-material and uncircumscribed, who has no form and is beyond comprehension; for how can that which is not seen be depicted? But, while no one has ever seen God, yet the only-begotten Son, who is in the bosom of the Father, has made this unseen God manifest (cf Jn 1:18)... And so with confidence I make an icon of the invisible God, not in so far as he is invisible, but in so far as he became visible for our sakes by partaking in flesh and blood... Israel of old did not see God, but we "with unveiled faces behold the glory of the Lord as though reflected in a mirror" (2 Cor 3:18).'[37]

What was impossible before the Incarnation has now become possible. Christ, the Word made flesh, is the 'icon of the invisible God' (Col 1:15) and so, by virtue of his Incarnation, we can make icons of him who is himself the Icon. In him 'the whole fulness of deity dwells bodily' (Col 2:9); perfect God has become entirely human, thereby enabling us to depict the human face of God. And if we can do so, then we must; otherwise we undermine our confession of the Saviour's true humanity.

2. The icon and the theology of creation

Our second point follows directly from the first. At the Incarnation God took a human body, using physical flesh as the means of our salvation. The Incarnation is unique; but, if God on this one occasion used matter as a vehicle of the Spirit, may it not serve as such on other occasions as well? 'God saw everything that he had made, and behold, it was altogether good and beautiful' (Gen 1:31, in the Greek Septuagint): all material things are intrinsically good and all therefore have Spirit-bearing potentialities. To this essential goodness and beauty of the material world the icon bears joyful and triumphant witness. In the icon we see matter restored to harmony and so fulfilling its true vocation, which is to be theophanic, to reflect and transmit the divine glory. The icon, then, safeguards not only the authenticity of Christ's physical body but equally the true value of all material things in their unfallen state, as created by God. Inherent in the art of the icon is an optimistic, affirmative vision of the material creation.

The upholders of the holy icons discerned in their opponents an over-intellectualist outlook, which despised matter and advocated an approach to God primarily through mental concepts. Without denying the use of the physical elements in the sacraments, the iconoclasts strove to reduce the 'materialism' of Christianity to a minimum. Matter they saw as shameful, inglorious, 'ignoble'; we insult Christ and the saints, so they maintained, when we depict them by means of 'worthless and dead matter'.[38] The iconodules or 'icon-venerators' vigorously repudiated this anti-materialist stance. Once more we may take St John of Damascus as spokesman of the Orthodox party:

'I do not worship matter, but I worship the creator of matter, who for my sake has become material, who has been pleased to dwell in matter and has through matter effected my salvation. I shall not cease to venerate matter, for it was through matter that my salvation came to pass... Do not insult matter, for it is no way despicable; nothing is despicable that God has made... Matter is filled with divine grace.'[39]

As Spirit-bearing matter, the icon has an eschatological significance. It anticipates the final transfiguration of the cosmos at the last day, when the created world will be delivered from its present 'bondage to corruption' and will enter into 'the glorious liberty of the children of God' (Rom 8:21).

Because the icon testifies in this manner to the goodness and beauty of the physical world, the iconographer needs to choose his materials with the utmost care. There should be nothing spurious or shoddy in what he employs, but everything should possess purity and integrity. Only so will the icon that he makes be a veridical witness to the glory of matter.

This testimony of the icon to the spiritual value of material things has surely an urgent contemporary relevance. Today, more than ever before, we need the art of the icon, specifically because it is an ecological art. 'The earth, although without words, yet groans and cries aloud: "Why, all people, do you pollute me with so many evils?"'[40] As we struggle to surmount the present crisis in our relationship to nature, the icon can help us to recover a sense of cosmic reverence and cosmic wonder. Through the icon we can cleanse the doors of our perception and appreciate once more the intrinsic holiness of material objects. Regaining an iconic vision of the creation, we can begin to see each thing as a sacrament of the divine presence. We have not much time left for this ecological *metanoia*; in many ways it is already too late...

3. The icon and the human person

As well as safeguarding the true doctrine of the Incarnation and of the creation, the icon shows us also what it means to be a human person in the image and likeness of God. Christ is the Icon of God (Col 1:15); we humans are created *kat'eikona*, in or according to his image (Gen 1:26), and by virtue of this fact we have the power to make artistic icons. The icon, that is to say, discloses to us our true human vocation as 'icons of the Icon'. By virtue of the divine image within us, we are each called to act as 'sub-creator' and cosmic priest; and that is precisely what we are doing whenever we make an icon.

The Byzantine sources from the period of the iconoclast controversy, while they speak at length about the Christological significance of the icon and about the value of the material creation, make very little reference to this third dimension in the theology of the icon. It is, however, at least implicit in a sentence by St Theodore the Studite: 'The fact that human beings are created in the image and likeness of God shows that the act of making an icon is in some way a divine action.'[41] Let us try to unpack the meaning of this epigrammatic phrase. When we make an icon, we take material elements such as wood, plaster or stone – in which, as we have just stated, the glory of God is already present – and then, using the creative powers inherent in us by virtue of the divine image, we render this glory manifest in a fuller and more explicit way. We do not simply recognize God's presence in the world, but we reveal it. In so making an icon, we are doing something that evinces the very essence of our human personhood, something that the other animals cannot do. With conscious awareness and deliberate choice we reshape creation, setting upon it the seal of our own intelligence and understanding. We indue it with fresh meaning, humanizing it and so offering it back to God the Creator. Just as in the Eucharist we bring to the altar not just sheaves of wheat and bunches of grapes, but bread and wine – not just the fruits of the earth in their original state, but the fruits of the earth transformed by human hands – so it is also in icon-painting. According to St Athanasius of Alexandria (c. 296-373), each human being made in the divine image is a creator after the likeness of God the Creator;[42] each, in J.R.R.Tolkein's phrase, is a 'sub-creator'.[43] Iconography, then, is an outstanding example of this 'sub-creation' that renders us characteristically human.

The iconographer serves in this way as priest of the creation, providing material things with a voice and so enabling them to glorify God. In the words of Gervase Mathew, 'The sound in a Byzantine hymn, the gestures in a liturgy, the bricks in a church, the cubes in a mosaic are matter made articulate in the Divine praise.'[44] As St Leontios of Cyprus affirms, in words that apply *par excellence* to the iconographer: 'The creation does not venerate the Maker directly through itself, but it is through me that the heavens declare the glory of God, through me the moon worships God, through me the waters and the showers of rain, the dew and all creation, venerate God and give him glory.'[45]

The icon thus brings together and illustrates three primary themes in our Christian faith: the reality of the Incarnation, the intrinsic goodness of the material creation and the dignity of the human person as fashioned in God's image. We can now begin to appreciate why, for the Orthodox Church, the icon is not peripheral, not an optional extra or a piece of unnecessary decoration, but an indispensable part of the 'rational worship' (Rom 12:1) by which we approach the living God.

Inverted Perspective

There is, however, one final point, the most important point of all, which has not as yet been sufficiently emphasized. The icon changes us; it makes us different. Between us and the icon there is, as it were, a two-way movement; we from our side offer veneration; the icon for its part transmits sanctifying grace. At an earlier stage, drawing on St John of Damascus, we cited St Paul's words, 'All of us, with unveiled faces, behold the glory of the Lord as though reflected in a mirror' (2 Cor 3:18). Let us continue the quotation: 'And so we are transformed into this same image (*eikon*) from one degree of glory to another.' The art of the icon is not only a liturgical art, a theological and contemplative art; it is also a transforming or transfiguring art. As a means of grace, conveying sanctifying power, the icon alters our consciousness and our spiritual state. It communicates *theosis*, 'deification' or 'divinization', to our created human nature. Without ceasing to be created, we participate through the icon in divine light and glory.

This aspect of the icon, as a centre of power that sanctifies and transforms us, is expressed by a particular feature in Orthodox iconography which often puzzles the Western beholder: the use of 'inverted' or 'reverse' perspective. In the art of the Western Renaissance, objects grow smaller the further they are from the spectator. In many icons, although not in all, the opposite happens: the more distant things are, the larger they become. A notable example of this is the icon of the Holy Trinity painted by St Andrew Rublov. The reason for this iconographic *metanoia*, to use Paul Evdokimov's phrase,[46] is nowhere explained in the Byzantine or the medieval Russian sources, but it has been discussed by several modern writers.[47] Briefly, its effect is to place the beholder *inside the picture*.

In Western painting, at the rear of the picture there is a vanishing point where the lines of perspective converge. But in the case of an icon there is no such imaginary vanishing point at the back. The lines pass out from the front of the picture and converge at the point where the viewer is standing. As a result we are not gazing in from the outside, as in a Renaissance work of art, but we are ourselves drawn into the scene and made part of it. We are not outside but inside. We and the figures in the icon are both within the same space. The icon is in this way converted into a place of meeting: the persons depicted in the icon come out from it to greet us and we on our side enter the scene, becoming not merely spectators but participants. We are directly involved; between us and the persons in the icon there is an immediate relationship, a bond of mutual communication.

Praying with icons, then, we no longer remain the same as we were before, but we are 'transformed into this same image from one degree of glory to another'. As we gaze in our worship upon the transfigured cosmos of the icon, we actually enter within that new world, becoming one with that which we behold, filled with its grace and changed by its power. The purpose of the icon is thus not only contemplation but transforming union. In T.S.Eliot's words, 'You are the music while the music lasts.'

NOTES

1. *Theology of the Icon* (St Vladimir's Seminary Press: New York, 1978), p. 10. This work, and also the book written jointly by Leonid Ouspensky and Vladimir Lossky, *The Meaning of Icons* (revised edition, St Vladimir's Seminary Press: New York, 1982), remain the best studies available in English on the Orthodox understanding of the icon. For a brief but perceptive initiation, see John Baggley, *Doors of Perception – icons and their spiritual significance* (Mowbray: London/Oxford, 1987). On the iconoclast controversy, consult Jaroslav Pelikan, *Imago Dei: The Byzantine Apologia for Icons* (Yale University Press: New Haven/ London, 1990). In French, see especially Paul Evdokimov, *L'art de l'icône. Théologie de la beauté* (Desclée de Brouwer: Bruges, 1970; an English translation was issued recently by Oakwood Publications, Redondo Beach, California, but this I have not yet seen) and Leonid Ouspensky, *La théologie de l'icône dans l'Eglise orthodoxe* (Cerf: Paris, 1980).
2. 'The Art of the Icon', in A. M. Allchin (ed.), *Sacrament and Image. Essays in the Christian Understanding of Man* (The Fellowship of St Alban and St Sergius: London, 1967), p. 58. Compare P. Sherrard, *The Sacred in Life and Art* (Golgonooza Press: Ipswich, 1990), p. 72.
3. 'On the Icon', *Eastern Churches Review* 8:1 (1976), p. 26.
4. *The 'Painter's Manual' of Dionysius of Fourna,* tr. Paul Hetherington (Sagittarius Press: London, 1974), p. 4.
5. E. Duchesne, *Le Stoglav ou les Cent Chapitres* (E. Champion: Paris, 1920), pp. 133-134.
6. *The 'Painter's Manual',* p. 4.
7. The practical techniques of icon-painting are described by Egon Sendler, *The Icon: Image of the Invisible* (Oakwood Publications: Redondo Beach, 1988).
8. Quoted in Eugene N. Trubetskoi, *Icons: Theology in Color* (St Vladimir's Seminary Press: New York, 1973), p. 72.
9. Daniel J. Sahas, *Icon and Logos: Sources in Eighth-Century Iconoclasm* (University of Toronto Press: Toronto, 1986), pp. 97-99.
10. The Russian rite has been translated by Mother Thekla, *The Blessing of Ikons* (Orthodox Monastery of the Assumption, Library of Orthodox Thinking, Pamphlet No 7: Normanby, n.d.). It is not easy to say how far back the practice of blessing icons extends, but a prayer is certainly to be found in the *Euchologion* of the Dominican Jacques Goar, first published in Paris in 1647; see the second edition (Venice, 1730), p. 672.
11. Migne, *PG [Patrologia Graeca]*, vol. 100, col. 1113A.
12. *On Icons* iii, 41 (ed. Bonifatius Kotter [Walter de Gruyter: Berlin, 1975], p. 143; tr. David Anderson, *St John of Damascus: On the Divine Images* [St Vladimir's Seminary Press: New York, 1980], p. 89; the English translation here, as often, requires correction). John is citing St Basil the Great, *On the Holy Spirit* xviii (45).
13. *L'art de l'icône*, p. 153.
14. 'On the Icon', pp. 16-17.

15. *On the Holy Temple* 236 (*PG* 155, 345CD).
16. Sahas, *Icon and Logos*, p. 99.
17. *Letter to Platon on the veneration of the holy icons* (*PG* 99, 505B).
18. *The Lenten Triodion*, tr. Mother Mary and Kallistos Ware (Faber & Faber: London, 1978), p. 300; *Triodion Katanyktikon* (Apostoliki Diakonia: Athens, 1960), p. 145.
19. Sahas, *Icon and Logos*, p. 179.
20. *Ibid.*, p. 96.
21. Theophanes Continuatus, *Chronographia* iii, 6 (ed. I. Bekker [Bonn, 1838], pp. 91-92); cf Edward James Martin, *A History of the Iconoclastic Controversy* (The Church Historical Society: London, n.d. [1930]), p. 210.
22. Illustrated in Steven Runciman, *Byzantine Style and Civilization* (Penguin Books: Harmondsworth, 1975), p. 101. But it is not easy to find other such examples: ivory reliefs are common in Byzantine art, free-standing ivory statues are not.
23. Evagrius of Pontus (d. 399), *On Prayer* 60 [61] (*PG* 79, 1180B); in *The Philokalia*, tr. G. E. H. Palmer, Philip Sherrard and Kallistos Ware, vol. i (Faber & Faber: London/Boston, 1979), p. 62.
24. Sahas, *Icon and Logos*, pp. 178-179.
25. *On Icons* i, 17 (Kotter, p. 93; Anderson, p. 25).
26. H. Denzinger and A. Schönmetzer, *Enchiridion Symbolorum* (ed. 36; Herder: Barcelona, 1976), nos. 653-654.
27. Robin Cormack, *Writing in Gold: Byzantine Society and its Icons* (George Philip: London, 1985).
28. Quoted in St John of Damascus, *On Icons* i, 56 (Kotter, p. 159; Anderson, p. 44). On the major importance of Leontios as a defender of the icon prior to the iconoclast controversy, see Norman H. Baynes, 'The Icons before Iconoclasm', in *Byzantine Studies and Other Essays* (The Athlone Press: London, 1955), pp. 226-239; Nicholas Gendle, 'Leontius of Neapolis: A Seventh Century Defender of Holy Images', in *Studia Patristica* xviii, 1 (Cistercian Publications: Kalamazoo, 1985), pp. 135-139.
29. *Against Constantine Cabalinus* (*PG* 95, 352C) (previously attributed to John of Damascus).
30. Ouspensky, *La théologie de l'icône*, p. 63.
31. 'On the Icon', p. 22.
32. Sahas, *Icon and Logos*, p. 84.
33. 'On the Icon', p. 18.
34. *The Sacred in Life and Art*, pp. 80-82.
35 The story is mentioned by the sixth-century historian Evagrius Scholasticus, *Church History* iv, 27, and used by St John of Damascus, *On Icons* i, 33 (Kotter, p. 145; Anderson, p. 35). Compare the Western story of St Veronica.
36. Sahas, *Icon and Logos*, p. 178.
37. *On Icons* ii, 5 and 7; i, 4 and 16 (Kotter, pp. 71, 74, 78, 92; Anderson, pp. 52, 54-55, 16, 25).
38. Sahas, *Icon and Logos*, p. 105; Cyril Mango, *The Art of the Byzantine Empire 312-1453* (Prentice-Hall: Englewood Cliffs, 1972), p. 168.

39. *On Icons* i, 16 and 36 (Kotter, pp. 89-90, 148; Anderson, pp. 23-24, 36).
40. From the 'Service in Danger of Earthquake', in the *Great Euchologion*: quoted in *Orthodoxy and the Ecological Crisis* (The Ecumenical Patriarchate, in co-operation with the World Wide Fund for Nature International: Gland, 1990), p. 10.
41. *Refutation* III, ii, 5 (*PG* 99, 420A; tr. Catharine P. Roth, *On the Holy Icons* [St Vladimir's Seminary Press: New York, 1981], p. 101).
42. *On the Decrees of the Council of Nicaea* xi, 1-2.
43. *Tree and Leaf* (Allen and Unwin: London, 1964), pp. 25, 36.
44. *Byzantine Aesthetics* (John Murray: London, 1963), p. 24.
45. *PG* 93, 1604B.
46. *L'art de l'icône*, p. 191.
47. See, for example, Ouspensky, *La théologie de l'icône*, pp. 469-472; Otto Demus, *Byzantine Mosaic Decoration* (Routledge & Kegan Paul: London, 1948), pp. 33-34; Boris Uspensky, *The Semiotics of the Russian Icon* (Peter de Ridder Press Publications in Semiotics of Art 3: Lisse, 1976), pp. 31-47.

Contributors

Sister Pamela Hayes RSCJ is a member of the Society of the Sacred Heart. After many years in Higher Education as Principal Lecturer in Religious Studies at St Mary's College, Newcastle-upon-Tyne, she is now engaged in a ministry of spiritual direction and retreats, and is based in The Sacred Heart Centre of Spirituality, Marden Lodge, Marden Park, Woldingham, Surrey, CR3 7YA.

Canon Hugh Wybrew is an Anglican priest who, as a student, spent a year at the Orthodox Institute of St Sergius in Paris and then, as Anglican chaplain, was for two years in Romania, Bulgaria and Yugoslavia. He was Dean of St George's Cathedral in Jerusalem from 1986 to 1989 and is currently Vicar of St Mary Magdalene, Oxford. He is a member of the International Commission for Anglican-Orthodox Theological Dialogue and the author of *The Orthodox Liturgy* (SPCK, London, 1989).

Father Paul McPartlan is a Catholic priest of the Diocese of Westminster. After reading Mathematics at Cambridge, he studied theology first in Rome and then at Oxford, where he gained his doctorate in 1990 with a thesis comparing the eucharistic ecclesiologies of Henri de Lubac and John Zizioulas: *The Eucharist Makes the Church. Henri de Lubac and John Zizioulas in dialogue* (T. & T. Clark, Edinburgh, 1992). He has written a number of articles on related topics and is currently Assistant Priest at Our Lady of Victories, Kensington.

Bishop Kallistos Ware became a member of the Orthodox Church in 1958 and has been Spalding Lecturer in Eastern Orthodox Studies in the University of Oxford since 1966. He is the titular Bishop of Diokleia, with pastoral responsibilities as assistant bishop in the Orthodox Archdiocese of Thyateira and Great Britain. Formerly the Orthodox theological secretary of the Anglican-Orthodox Joint Doctrinal Commission, his many publications include *The Orthodox Church* (new edition due in 1992) and *The Orthodox Way* (1979).

Appendix

LETTER OF HIS HOLINESS
POPE JOHN PAUL II
TO THE BISHOPS OF EUROPE
ON RELATIONS BETWEEN CATHOLICS AND
ORTHODOX IN THE NEW SITUATION OF
CENTRAL AND EASTERN EUROPE

Dear Brother Bishops,

As preparations for the forthcoming Special Assembly for Europe of the Synod of Bishops* intensify,
I would like to share with you my joy at the new
situation which is emerging in Central and Eastern
Europe in particular. I would also like to express my
hope for the new opportunities being presented for the
life of the Church in those regions. The effects and
positive developments on a world level of the changes
which have taken place in that part of the 'old Conti-
nent', the universal dimension of the episcopal ministry and the communion of all the Bishops with the
Successor of Peter all lead me to share with you some
reflections on the new situation and its consequences
with regard to relations between Catholics and members of the Orthodox Churches.

Changes in Central and Eastern Europe

1. Several peoples of Eastern Europe have recently
regained – by God's grace, without bloodshed – the

---

* This Special Assembly of delegates from Western, Eastern and Central
Europe discussed the evangelisation of Europe and was held in Rome
from 28 November to 15 December, 1991.

right to respect for civil liberties, including freedom of religion, which for decades in those lands had been limited, repressed or suppressed. These changes and advances are certainly the result of the intervention of God, who with wisdom and patience directs the course of history towards its eschatological goal: 'to unite all things in Christ' (Eph 1:10).

The climate of aversion to religious freedom and of open persecution has affected, in one form or other, all believers: Catholics, Orthodox, Protestants and members of other religions. Persecution reached its greatest intensity in the cases where, as in the Ukraine, Romania and Czechoslovakia, the local Catholic Churches of the Byzantine tradition were declared dissolved and non-existent by the use of authoritarian and devious methods. Pressure, sometimes of a violent nature, was put on Catholics to join the Orthodox Churches.

The recent laws on religious freedom seek to guarantee for all the possibility of legitimately expressing their faith, with their own structures and places of worship.

This positive new situation has thus made it possible to reorganise the Latin Rite Catholic Church in a number of nations and enabled the Byzantine Rite Catholic Churches to return to a normal life in countries where they had been suppressed. History is remedying an act of grave injustice. The Lord has granted me the grace of naming Bishops for those Byzantine Rite Churches in the Western Ukraine and in Romania. These Churches are now resuming the normal process of public Church life, emerging from the clandestine situation to which, sad to say, persecution had relegated them.

I have likewise been able to provide Bishops for various Latin sees which for years had remained empty. This makes possible an ordered growth of Church life. Bishops, as teachers of the faith and ministers of reconciliation, promote the harmonious growth of their churches; at the same time they develop fraternal relations with other believers in Christ with a view to the restoration of the full unity which he willed, and in this they carry out the norms established by the Second Vatican Council and repeated in the Code of Canons of the Oriental Churches: 'Especially, indeed, the pastors of the Church must pray and work for that fulness of unity desired by the Lord, participating diligently in ecumenical activity prompted by the Holy Spirit' (*CCEO*, Canon 902, trans. by editor; cf also *CIC*, Canon 755).

Tensions between Catholics and Orthodox in these Regions

2. But in the course of this process of the reorganisation of the Catholic Church, and also as a result of the wounds left by the painful experiences of the past, there has unfortunately been evidence of problems and tensions between Catholics and Orthodox, especially with regard to the ownership and use of places of worship which formerly belonged to Byzantine Rite Catholic Churches and which were later confiscated by the respective governments and, in part, handed over to the Orthodox Churches.

Disagreement over places of worship has also had negative repercussions within the theological dialogue between the Catholic Church and the Orthodox Church, which had been fruitfully pursuing its course for over ten years. Joint reflection on the demands which arise from fraternal coexistence, which ought to tend towards full ecclesial communion in accordance with the will of Christ for his Church, will help all concerned to find a solution that is fair and worthy of the Christian calling. Reparation for a past injustice can only help the positive development of mutual relations.

All must be convinced that also in cases such as these disputes over relatively contingent and practical matters, dialogue still remains the best instrument for embarking upon a fraternal exchange which aims at settling the issue in a spirit of justice, charity and forgiveness. Brothers who once shared the same sufferings and trials ought not to oppose one another today, but should look together at the future opening before them with promising signs of hope.

The Oriental Catholic Churches in other Parts of the World

3. The question of relations between Oriental Rite Catholics and Orthodox is not however limited to the countries of Eastern Europe, but, in different forms, also arises wherever Oriental Catholic Churches are present. In the Middle East in particular, in addition to the Churches of the Byzantine tradition, there also coexist the ancient Churches of the Alexandrian, Antiochene, Armenian and Chaldean traditions. Here the most recent events have revealed a special threat for the Catholic communities, which are generally small in numbers. By reason of the difficulties of those countries, often marked by lengthy and at times armed conflicts, emigration is becoming more and more frequent, and this brings in its wake increasing problems both for those who remain in their native country and for the Oriental communities being established abroad.

The spirit of mutual understanding and communion, guided by the words of Saint Paul who invites us to 'bear one another's burdens' (Gal 6:2), will help to resolve the objective difficulties existing both in the countries of origin and in those of the diaspora. This is especially necessary since in those areas Catholics and Orthodox often come from an identical ecclesial tradition and share a common ethnic and cultural heritage.

Bishops will be careful to ensure that dialogue in charity and truth inspires the reorganisation and the life of the Oriental Catholic Churches, in accordance with the detailed guidelines of the Second Vatican Council. The Bishops of the Catholic Church gathered at the Council declared, in the Decree on the Eastern Catholic Churches, that 'the Catholic Church highly esteems the institutions, liturgical rights, ecclesiastical traditions and way of Christian life of the Eastern Churches' and they expressed the hope that those Churches will 'flourish and fulfil with fresh apostolic vigour the task entrusted to them' (*Orientalium Ecclesiarum*, 1). To this end, the Council Fathers requested that 'steps be taken for the preservation' of all the particular Churches (*ibid.*, 4), and that suitable pastoral tools be placed at their disposal for carrying out the service which these Churches should provide for governing, educating and sanctifying their faithful, inasmuch as the liturgical, disciplinary and theological traditions of each of those Churches are 'more suited to the customs of their faithful and more suitable for assuring the good of souls' (*ibid.*, 5). This criterion and pastoral orientation will inspire the organisation of the structures of these Churches, the theological formation of their clergy, and the catechetical instruction of their faithful. Genuine pastoral service in fact consists of precisely this.

Concern for Christian Unity

4. The Second Vatican Council also taught that an integral part of the life of these Churches, as also of the whole Catholic Church, is the concern, particularly strong in them because of their origins, to promote the unity of Christians: 'The Oriental Churches in communion with the Apostolic See of Rome have a special role to play in promoting the unity of all Christians, particularly Oriental Christians, according to the principles of this Council's Decree on Ecumenism: first of all by prayer, then by the example of their lives, by religious fidelity to ancient Oriental traditions, by greater mutual knowledge, by collaboration, and by a brotherly regard for objects and attitudes.' (*ibid.*, 24)

This orientation was recently reaffirmed by the new Code of Canons of the Oriental Churches (cf *CCEO*, Canon 903).

In the complex history of the origin – differing in time and place – of these Churches, and independently of the influence of culture and politics, the desire to re-establish full ecclesial communion was certainly not lacking, in accordance, obviously, with the methods and sensitivities of the age. The conflicts which later arose have not cancelled out that prospect, even though they have sometimes obscured it. In our own time, the theological dialogue taking place between the Catholic Church and the Orthodox Churches as a body is directed towards that goal with a new method and with a different form and outlook, in accordance with the teachings and directives of the Second Vatican Council.

The Decree on Ecumenism, with a powerful expression full of theological meaning, recalled that 'through the celebration of the Eucharist of the Lord in each of these Churches, the Church of God is built up and grows in stature' (*Unitatis Redintegratio*, 15). Through the service of these Churches 'the faithful, united with their Bishop, gain access to God the Father, through the Son, the Word made flesh, who suffered and was glorified, in the outpouring of the Holy Spirit, and so are made "partakers of the divine nature" and enter into communion with the Most Holy Trinity' (*ibid.*). Hence with these Churches relations are to be fostered as between sister Churches, to use the expression of Pope Paul VI in his Brief to the Patriarch of Constantinople Athenagoras I (*Anno Ineunte*, 25 July 1967: *AAS* 59 [1967], 852-854).

The unity with these Churches which is sought – and must be sought – is full communion in one faith, in the sacraments and in ecclesial government (cf *Lumen Gentium*, 14), with full respect for legitimate liturgical, disciplinary and theological diversity, as I explained in my Apostolic Epistle *Euntes in Mundum Universum*, on the occasion of the Millennium of the Baptism of Kievan Rus' (25 January 1988, n.10: *AAS* 80 [1988], 949-950).

Pastoral Consequences

5. From this there follow immediate and practical consequences. The first of these was stated by Pope Paul VI in the Address which he gave in the Cathedral of the Ecumenical Patriarchate on the occasion of his visit, and it retains all of its validity today: 'Thus we see more clearly that it is incumbent upon the heads of the Churches and upon their hierarchy to lead the Churches along the path which leads to the

regaining of full communion. They must do so by recognising and respecting each other as pastors of the portion of the Lord's flock entrusted to them, by having care for the cohesion and growth of the people of God and by avoiding anything which could scatter it or sow confusion in its ranks' (25 July, 1967, *AAS* 59 [1967], 841; trans. by editor).

A second consequence is the rejection of all undue forms of proselytism, with the avoidance in the most absolute way in pastoral action of any temptation to violence and any form of pressure. At the same time, pastoral action will not fail to respect the freedom of conscience and the right which each individual has to join, if he wishes, the Catholic Church. In brief, it is a matter of respecting the action of the Holy Spirit, who is the Spirit of truth (cf Jn 16:13). The Council's Decree on Ecumenism stated this and gave the reason thus: 'it is evident that the work of preparing and reconciling those individuals who wish for full Catholic communion is of its nature distinct from ecumenical action. But there is no opposition between the two, since both proceed from the wondrous providence of God.' (*Unitatis Redintegratio*, 4)

The third consequence is that it is obviously not enough just to avoid mistakes: it is also necessary to promote positively coexistence with mutual and harmoniuous respect. This attitude has certainly been proposed and reaffirmed as the rule of conduct in relations between Catholics and Orthodox, as was stated by Pope Paul VI and the Patriarch Athenagoras I in their joint declaration: 'The dialogue of charity between their Churches must bear fruit in impartial collaboration in planning for common action on the pastoral, social and intellectual levels and in mutual respect for the fidelity of one another to their own

Churches.' (28 October 1967: AAS 59 [1967], 1055; trans. by editor). As I had occasion to state in my Encyclical *Slavorum Apostoli*, all this will help the mutual enrichment of the two great traditions, the Eastern and the Western, and the path towards full unity.

At the Service of Ecumenism

6. The Oriental Catholic Churches know and accept with an attitude of trust the teaching of the Second Vatican Council on ecumenism, and they intend to play their part in the search for full unity between Catholics and Orthodox. It is a source of joy to see that this fact is being given positive consideration in bilateral relations, as has happened in recent declarations.

It is my heartfelt hope that wherever Oriental Catholics and Orthodox live side by side there will be established relations which are fraternal, mutually respectful and sincerely seeking a common testimony to the one Lord. This will help not only coexistence in practical circumstances but will also facilitate the theological dialogue directed to overcoming whatever still divides Catholics and Orthodox. Being faithful witnesses to Jesus Christ who has set us free should be the main concern in our time of cultural, social and political changes, so that we can preach together and with credibility the one Gospel of salvation, and be builders of peace and reconciliation in a world always threatened by conflicts and wars.

Entrusting these sentiments and hopes to the intercession of the Virgin Theotokos, venerated both in the East and in the West, that as the Hodegitria she may guide all Christians on the path of the Gospel and of full communion, I gladly impart my special Apostolic Blessing to you, dear Brothers in the Episcopate, and to the communities entrusted to your care.

From the Vatican, 31 May 1991
Joannes Paulus PP. II

ONE LORD, ONE FAITH
ONE CHURCH

René Girault

The yearning for unity is one of the powerful forces the Holy Spirit has generated at the heart of Christianity in the twentieth century. But after some promising decades of ecumenism the efforts of the Churches at understanding and reconciliation seem to have ended without achieving full unity.

This book has been written in the conviction that new perspectives are being formed today. It traces the great ecumenical journey of the last six decades. The account shows how much has been achieved and also how much still remains to be done. The author believes that the time has come to focus on the 'genius' of each Church as it is only by mutual enrichment that the Churches can make progress on the road to unity.

This lucid and positive book is a true invitation to ecumenism, inspiring hope and faith in the future and rekindling the passion for unity in the hearts of all Christians as we approach the dawn of the new millennium.

RENÉ GIRAULT *is a priest of the diocese of Poitiers, France. He has been engaged in fostering ecumenical relations as Secretary of the Episcopal Commission for Christian Unity, Director of the National Secretariat for Ecumenism and Editor of the magazine* Unité des Chretiens.

160 pages   ISBN 085439 425 7   £6.95

CHURCH, ECUMENISM & POLITICS

Joseph Ratzinger

"The articles and papers collected here form a kind of second volume to the ecclesiological essays which I published in 1969 under the title *Das neue Volk Gottes*. The basic issues have remained the same: the question of the nature of the Church, its structure, the ecumenical scene, the relationship of the Church and the world. But in many cases the emphasis has shifted and new evaluations have become necessary.

The debate about Christian ecumenism and efforts to achieve the right relationship of faith and politics occupy the foreground of the reflections that make up this volume. Some of the contributions reprinted here aroused vigorous debate when they were first published, and I have tried to do justice to this debate either in additional footnotes or in newly added postscripts. I hope that in this way it will become clear that these essays are meant as a contribution to dialogue with the aim that by listening to each other we shall be able to hear more clearly Him who in His person is the word and truth."

JOSEPH RATZINGER:*born in 1927; Professor of Theology in the Universities of Bonn, Münster, Tübingen and Regensburg; peritus at the Second Vatican Council; Archbishop of Munich (1977); since 1981 Prefect of the Sacred Congregation for the Doctrine of the Faith.*

278 pages   ISBN 085439 267 X   £9.95

IN SEARCH OF UNITY
Ecumenical principles and prospects
Edward Yarnold

"Ecumenical principles and prospects" in the light of the past two decades of Anglican-Roman Catholic dialogue is the theme of this book by one of Britain's foremost theologians. In many ways the gap between Canterbury and Rome seems wider now than when it all began. The road to unity is harder to map than was imagined in the post-Vatican II ecumenical optimism. And yet the ecumenical commitment remains: there is no turning back.

Fr Yarnold here outlines the challenges that confront, at every turn, the efforts towards unity, showing how to overcome some of the apparently insurmountable difficulties and how to break new grounds in Christ's footsteps.

EDWARD YARNOLD *is tutor at Campion Hall and Chairman of the Oxford University Faculty of Theology. He is the author of several books such as* The Theology of Original Sin, The Awe-inspiring Rites of Initiation, The Second Gift, They are in earnest *and numerous articles.*

132 pages   ISBN 085439 309 9   £5.75

GROWING CLOSER TOGETHER
Rome and Canterbury: a relationship of hope

Maria J. Van Dyck

A clear, simple, yet scholarly account of the events that led
the English Church to break away from Rome and of the
various ecumenical efforts and movements since to heal the
rift. After examining the forces and factors that caused the
English Church's break with Rome, the book studies the
relationship between Anglicans and Catholics from the 16th
to the 20th century, then focuses on the ARCIC statement
'Authority in the Church' (1976-1982) and its significance
for Anglican-Catholic dialogue in the present century.

As Henry Chadwick says in his foreword to the book,
historical method alone cannot bring about reconciliation
where fundamental dogma is at stake. Yet without an
awareness of the past debates there can be no real progress
in dialogue. This awareness is what Maria Van Dyck offers
the reader, which ends with the image of Pope John Paul II
and Archbishop Robert Runcie praying together – a symbol
of the sharing of love and authority in the hoped for one
Church of Christ.

*MARIA J. VAN DYCK is a member of the Canonical Order of the
Holy Sepulchre in Turnhout Priory (Belgium). She is a Doctor of
Sciences in Zoology and a lector emeritus of the Catholic University of Louvain where she graduated in Theology and obtained a
doctorate in 1989 for her dissertation 'Church and Authority'.
Since 1989 she has been giving lectures in ecumenical subjects
throughout Belgium.*

267 pages   ISBN 085439 402 8   £9.95

THINGS OLD AND NEW

*An ecumenical reflection
on the theology of John Henry Newman*

Emmanuel Sullivan

Things old and new shows in a clear and convincing way how the three characteristic elements in Newman's thinking about the tradition of the Church, the development of doctrine and the need to consult the faithful can be keys to understanding contemporary puzzles on the ecumenical agenda. What it says about receiving the fruits of ecumenical dialogue in the life of our Churches and about the approach to the question of the ordination of women is helpful and healing. Its great contribution lies in the insights it gives to the ecumenical pilgrimage in the last decade of this century. If these ecumenical lessons drawn from Newman's writings can be learnt we shall continue together, Anglicans and Roman Catholics, within the wider ecumenical movement towards the visible unity of the one, holy, catholic and apostolic Church.

EMMANUEL SULLIVAN *is a Franciscan Friar of the Atonement. Since 1967 he has been active in ecumenical ministry. and helped establish an ecumenical community and centre at Hengrave Hall in Suffolk. He was a visiting scholar at St Edmund's House, Cambridge. In 1984 he became director of the Graymoor Ecumenical Institute. Recently he has been appointed ecumenical officer to the RC Diocese of Arundel and Brighton.*

160 pages   ISBN 085439 438 9   £6.95

MARY'S PLACE
IN CHRISTIAN DIALOGUE

Edited by Alberic Stacpoole

During the last two decades the Christian world has been in unprecedented decline. Fewer believe in Jesus Christ as Son of God, and fewer still practise their beliefs. Christians, however, accepting this sad recession have never ceased pursuing what St Anselm called *fides quaerens intellectum*, belief in search of understanding. Part of that search has been to understand other Christian confessions or traditions more deeply and more appreciatively.

Nowhere is this more evident than in Mariology, pursuit of the truth concerning the Mother of God. Nowhere has that been more fruitful than in the Ecumenical Society of the Blessed Virgin Mary; and nowhere there more effectively than in the addresses delivered to the Society by its members (from bishops to laymen). A representative gathering of these papers is published here.

281 pages ISBN 085439 201 7 H/b £10.00